LIKE THE O

Books by Samuel Southard
Published by The Westminster Press

LIKE THE ONE YOU LOVE
Intimacy and Equality in Modern Marriage

ANGER IN LOVE

PEOPLE NEED PEOPLE

THE FAMILY AND MENTAL ILLNESS

LIKE THE ONE YOU LOVE

Intimacy and Equality in Modern Marriage

by

SAMUEL SOUTHARD

THE WESTMINSTER PRESS • PHILADELPHIA

PUBLISHED BY THE WESTMINSTER PRESS®
PHILADELPHIA, PENNSYLVANIA

PRINTED IN THE UNITED STATES OF AMERICA

Library of Congress Cataloging in Publication Data

Southard, Samuel.
Like the one you love.

Includes bibliographical references.
1. Marriage—United States. 2. Family—United States. I. Title.
HQ536.S68 301.42′0973 73–21966
ISBN 0–664–24986–8

To our marriage arrangers,
Aaron and Stella Rutledge

and to Pamela,
who recommended from her college courses
in mental health the articles and books
that are basic for this manuscript

Contents

Introduction

> Dr. Laura Singer, past president of the American Association of Marriage Counselors, told a New York audience that divorces are skyrocketing. Between a third and a quarter of all marriages end in divorce. The old religious tenet of "till death do us part" has disintegrated. Today, couples want marriage to serve the self. People are searching desperately for new religious meaning in marriage. (TV news story, Feb. 24, 1973.)

Can a middle-class marriage survive the modern requirements of *self*-fulfillment? Couples are now looking for "undependent" living, individual freedom, "expansion through openness." These and other phrases characterize a new life-style, a philosophy of flexible roles and multiple options for sex and companionship.

The January, 1972, issue of *Psychology Today* featured a conversation with Robert Rimmer about group marriage and other loving arrangements. Mr. Rimmer had just finished a novel called *Thursday My Love* which proposes a structured form of open-end monogamy. He looks forward to the day of socially approved group marriages, bigamous marriages, and open-end marriages in which each partner has a relationship outside the marriage. Mr. Rimmer has received hundreds of letters from people experimenting with alternative approaches to marriage and the family. He hopes for a church-sanctioned marital relationship that would allow adultery by consent of both parties and a second supplemental marriage if necessary. He believes that ultimately the church has got to come to grips with alternative life-styles particularly when they support a strong family structure. Men need something to lean on. The church can continue to be strong but can show new vitality in the sanction of synergamy.

Germaine Greer, author of *The Female Eunuch,* told *Playboy* (January, 1972) that she is passionately opposed to the nuclear family. She thinks it is a neurotic life-style. The mother and the children are too close. The husband is unnecessary and increases the tension between mother and children. The neuroticism is compounded by the institution of marriage. Institutions spoil warmth and spontaneity. The contract of marriage is one of the worst forms of law. The answer for Ms. Greer is group cohabitation.

Mr. Rimmer and Ms. Greer recommend radical shifts in the institution of marriage. Other persons adopt a less aggressive approach and drop out of marriage.

The March, 1972, issue of *Life* featured a "Dropout Wife." Thirty-five-year-old Wanda Lee Adams, college graduate, wife of a middle-level Seattle executive, and mother of three walked out on her family in the summer of 1971. She wanted to begin a new life on her own. There was no great animosity or dramatic grievance. By most standards the fourteen-year marriage was a success. Her husband was considered attentive and devoted. Money was not a factor. The problem was that after about ten years of marriage Wanda Adams began to see her life as frustrating and suffocating. She went back to school and encountered the Women's Liberation Movement. Then she saw that her husband had allowed her to grow to a certain point but beyond that point she had to leave.

The editors interviewed marriage counselors, psychiatrists, and detective agencies around the country to confirm the growth of the dropout-wife phenomenon. Most dropouts are middle-class, educated, highly motivated women who have been married a number of years.

A New Prescription for an Old Institution

Can marriage be reevaluated in modern society and maintain necessary functions as the primary source of companionship for man and woman, the reliable source of sexual fulfillment, reproduction, and child nurture?

We can keep the functions if we change some assumptions. The old marital assumptions were ownership of the mate and denial of self. The new culture stresses equality for the female and self-actualization of both partners.

A plan for new life-styles must balance commitment to a mate with fulfillment of the self. More specifically, there must be equality of the sexes. Men and women must be intimate friends who find in each other the qualities that they enjoy in themselves. Mutual admiration is mixed with sexual affection and social responsibility. The result is a formula: Like the one you love.

This prescription may sound too obvious. Certainly we will expect to like the person we marry! But when we question people about marriage, we find that they make some distinctions between the explanations of "like" and "love." "Like" is the enjoyment found in doing things together, in mutual respect and in fulfillment. "Love" is more connected to sentimentality, sexual attraction, the giving and receiving of affection.

In common usage, "like" is the term of affection for a friend and "love" is the term for endearment of a mate. The former is usually associated with equality, while the latter may or may not have that meaning. In popular song and novel "love" is the longing for the reduction of tension through sexual conquest, which is graphically portrayed as the surrender of the female to the desires of the male. This is the over-under relationship that is bitterly resented by modern women and rejected by mature men.

To stress the current emphasis upon equality and self-affirmation, I have used "like" for friendship and "love" for the sentiment of desire and dominance. When the two come together we have a new form of love, one in which erotic fulfillment and responsibility for children are fused with the response of equals to mutually satisfying goals.

In the chapters that follow we will consider the implications of this formula for new life in marriage. We will find that many of the assumptions are not new; they go back to the writings of Aristotle or of Shakespeare on the subject of friendship. The application is new. This is the first time in Western civilization that the married relationship could be based on friendship. The basic definition of *philia* is an intimate tie of *equals*. The last half of the twentieth century has created conditions under which men and women could expect and could accomplish this relationship of peers.

Remember also the definition of a prescription. It is a remedy offered after diagnosis. A prescription is specifically for one person and not for any other. Today, the formula of "Like the one you love" is directed toward a troubled group of middle-class people, many of them educated and talented women who feel closed in by traditional matrimony. The incidence is increasing of matrons who tell a marriage counselor: "I married young and didn't know what I was doing. Now I've completed my education and have (or want) a good job. I really can't talk to my husband anymore. I want out!"

The prescription is also aimed at the middle-aged man or woman who now realizes that he (she) does not *have* to stay married. Divorce is now decent. Marriage may seem less attractive as the man or woman measures the spouse and finds that he (she) is really *not* equal. What then? This is the case of Mr. Gaston (see Chapter 2).

I would write a different prescription for couples who know they are unequal, or who don't know it and seem to be well adjusted. I would suggest some of the same ingredients that are found in the following chapters: faith, hope, love. But the dosage would be different. Instead of 50-50 every day, I would recommend one role in which he is 75 percent and she is 25 percent, another in which she is 75 percent and he 25 percent. I would include relationships in which self-denial and ownership were prominent.

The difference is dependency. Dependent people can be satisfied in marriage, but not if they are expected to perform on the level of Dr. Abraham Maslow's "self-actualized" individual. They find as much fulfillment as they can in an intimate relationship, and use the traditional roles of marriage to shelter their inadequacies. Of course, no prescription need be written for those who are well. Many adequate persons are happy with traditional ties. They like their roles as husband and wife, which have come down, with slight alterations only, through the centuries.

The present book is for those who are alive to the possibilities of change in modern institutions and who feel adequate to cope with the responsibilities of a new way of life. If you are or if you hope to be ready for an intimate relationship based on equality, then you can define marriage as an enduring friendship: you'll "like" the one you love.

1

Possess Yourself

We like the one we love when there is mutual joy of accomplishment. This does not have to be work side by side, or attendance at the same sports, or participation in similar hobbies. Tastes may differ without loss of respect. Modern couples do not "need" each other all day—and there are many nights when they are apart.

The mutual joy of accomplishment is an inner feeling that we like what we do and that the one we love has admiration and respect for our activities. We can "do our own thing" without turning to our partner for approval or guidance. All we need is the knowledge of another's acceptance of our judgment and joy in the tasks of life.

Equalitarian marriage means happiness in self-possession. We are the kind of person and do the kind of things that satisfy us—and our partner is happy because we are. For the man, the self-satisfaction may be very concrete: a salary check, an invention, an election to some useful office. The woman may achieve satisfaction in interpersonal skills such as rearing the children, understanding her husband, cooperating with the neighbors.

But many of these relationship skills seem less significant in our day of early kindergarten for the children and interpersonal relationship workshops for husbands in business or industry. Wisdom in "working things out" is no longer a feminine distinctive.

Will the sharing of skills lead past autonomy to isolation of husband from wife? The autonomy would be desirable, but the isolation destroys both friendship and love. So far as modern studies can show, there is still a good deal of mutual support in marriage; individuality has not yet broken down into insulated husband and lonely wife.

In 1961 interviews were conducted with 1,811 wives in 17 Chicago suburbs. As predicted, the traditional power of the husband was diminishing. At the same time, he was sharing more in the relationship problems of the family. But he was still the technical expert, the manipulator of the environment for the sake of his family's economic well-being. The wife was still the cultural expert, the human relations mediator for the family.[1]

Many women are still quite content to be "possessed," even though the desire for self-sufficiency is being stressed in modern society. In a study of women in New York City, in Lima, Peru, and in Buenos Aires, there was substantial agreement on the questionnaire "Inventory of Female Values." The women felt that they should be subordinate, that the husband should be looked up to, that marital success was more important than personal fame. They believed that men want women to be listeners, that it is not desirable to be a leader, that they should put themselves in the background. Motherhood was worth what it costs to them, and there was no conflict as they experienced womanhood and individuality.[2]

This is data for the caution expressed in the Introduction: equality is not for everyone. A friendship marriage is a specific prescription for the talented, troubled group of middle-class and upper-middle-class people who feel closed in by the traditional views of dominant-subordinate matrimony.

If we measure equality by economic opportunity, society has not moved very far. In fact, Mrs. Koontz, head of the Women's Bureau in the Department of Labor, found a widening gap in male-female pay. A woman working full time in 1970 made only 57 percent of a man's income, down from 64 percent in 1955.[3]

There is also a lack of legal recognition for women as the equal of men in such diverse areas as marriageable age, age of majority, jury service, criminal-sentencing, hours limitations, minimum wage laws, actions for loss of consortium, name after marriage, contracts and property rights, alimony, support, grounds for divorce. Lee Kanowitz has called these problems an "unfinished revolution" in his study *Women and the Law.*[4]

Despite the lag in law and salary, social forces are moving toward the possibility of equalitarian marriage. The battle for equal pay is being won, equal employment opportunities are enforced in state and federal government, educational levels for women rise, and household labor decreases.

Of even greater importance for joy in self-possession is the concept of woman as an independent person; she no longer must find fulfillment in surrender to a man.

Nena and George O'Neill have traced the development of feminine adequacy in their book *Open Marriage*. They found the 1950's and 1960's to be the era of the wife, mother, teacher, and mistress. One popular writer, George Lawton, stressed twenty-five roles for wives in a 1956 article on "Emotional Maturity in Wives." Dr. Helen Deutsch elaborated the Freudian doctrine of feminine deficiency into a positive rationale for passivity and dependency. A woman was to keep the man at home by being an excellent mistress. She was to develop deep inwardness and readiness for the final goal of sexual life which was impregnation.

Dr. Marie Robinson wrote in 1959 on *The Power of Sexual Surrender*. Women were to cultivate excitement in the act of surrender. If not, they alone were responsible for frigidity in marriage. Her goal for women was vaginal orgasm.

In the 1960's the research of Masters and Johnson explored the myth of vaginal orgasm in *Human Sexual Response* (1966) and *Human Sexual Inadequacy* (1970). Their research placed responsibility for sexual fulfillment upon both partners.

The O'Neills captured the mood of the 1970's in their emphasis upon life as a cooperative venture. The needs of each partner are to be fulfilled without an overriding dependency that cripples the self-expression of the other. They contrasted traditional (closed) and equalitarian (open) marriage:

Closed Marriage	*Open Marriage*
ownership of the mate	undependent living
denial of the self	personal growth
couples game of always being like each other	individual freedom
rigid role behavior	flexible roles
absolute fidelity	mutual trust
enforced togetherness	expansion through openness[5]

In later chapters we will evaluate some of these contrasts; for the present it is enough to observe the popularity of this and related titles on best-seller lists. The theory of equality is growing and the assumptions of marriage are changing. Now it's possible to like as an equal the one you also love.

The Anxieties of Autonomy

But we do not change institutional moorings without anxiety. In the current reevaluation of marriage there are challenges to child-rearing practices, changes in parental supervision over courtship, liberal assumptions about premarital conduct, anxiety over adequate performance as an equal in marriage.

Women still thrive on primary group relationships. Structured interviews with fifty-one husbands and wives in a working-class suburb of the Twin Cities showed feminine dissatisfaction with upward mobility. Why? Because family ties were disrupted. Relatives and friends were left behind in the inner city. The husband thought that the family had "bettered itself" in a flight to the suburbs, but the wife was lonely and miserable.[6]

People are not only shaken by physical distance, they are apprehensive about the social chasm between generations. Rites of passage from childhood to adulthood are being revised, or abolished.

The old bridges between generations are down. Church and school do not enforce parental dominance, chaperons and dating parlors have disappeared from college campuses, protective laws and customs for women are being challenged.

The evidence for openness to change is strong. We may not have moved very far from our own mores, but we are much more tolerant of deviance on the part of others. Also, we are more willing to try something different ourselves . . . sometime.

From a predominately liberal-minded audience, *Psychology Today* found that only 16 percent of 20,000 respondents "might be interested" in wife-swapping through group marriage. Less than half of the 20,000 disapproved such arrangements. The mood is of tolerance—and curiosity. Only 5 percent participated in wife-swapping, but over half of the men (and one fifth of the women) "might consider it." [7]

The respondents rejected any philosophy of a double standard:

> Fewer than one percent believe that men may have sexual freedom but women may not. They agree that women should feel free to initiate sexual activity ("except when the poor guy's exhausted," one woman added). And they disagree with a view, common in some groups, that a woman should pretend to be sexually naïve at the time of marriage, even if she is sexually experienced.[8]

But there are some anxieties that accompany the open and adventurous approach to marriage. One girl wrote: "My body is pretty uninhibited. My psyche is tied up in knots." An older woman wrote that her "prudish" upbringing caused many hang-ups in her failing marriage. Another explained that there were still some ghosts from the past that surprised husband and wife, even though they agreed on sexual freedom.[9]

The current emphasis upon self-fulfillment has centered so much on sex that Rollo May has written: "The contemporary age has singled out sex as its chief concern and required sex to carry the weight of all forms of love." The result is "so much sex and so little meaning or even fun in it!" The push for adequacy of technique increases insecurity: "The partner pants and quivers hoping to find an answering quiver in someone else." [10]

A Friendly Source of Security

The dilemma of modern marriage is security-insecurity. On the one hand, traditional marriage offers security but with assumptions from an age that is past. On the other hand, intimate relationships without guarantees create insecurity. What kind of tie can bind people together without violating individuality?

The most stable and creative relationship between equals is friendship. This can be the guiding principle for modern marriage. Sociologically, it has been demonstrated in Blood and Wolfe's questionnaire to 900 women in Detroit. "Companionship in doing things together" was the most valuable aspect of their marriage. "Love" was a poor second, followed by "understanding," "standard of living," "chance to have children."

Historically, friendship has been the only intimate relationship between equals. From the days of Confucius and Plato to Luther and Calvin, all other ties were between superior and subordinate. Friendship is the classical model for remolding the last inequality, marriage, on a democratic base.

Philosophically, Tillich and others have defined *philia* (friendship) as the only lasting relationship of affection between men of equality. Now that principle will be applied man to woman.

The principles of friendship have special relevance for the challenges of modern marriage. First, friendship is based on deliberate choice, which is also the volitional assumption of modern engagement. "Arranged" marriages are antiquated. Second, the characteristics of the friend must be valued as highly as are those of the self. There is no thought of making up for a lack in another, finding protection, or enjoying dominance. We find pleasure in the friend because he represents that which is permanent in us (Aristotle). Third, the fidelity of friends is based on mutual admiration rather than on social convention. Our inner values are the guarantee of a fixed relationship.

Fourth, the most noble act of friendship was the sharing of possessions and, if required, of life itself. Shakespeare considered the Merchant of Venice to be noble because he would give his own flesh as surety for his friend.

Fifth, in the marketplace economy of modern society, possessions are the barometer of our relationships. What do we think about money, property, status, education? These are the values of the technocrat, who hardly remembers his roots in family, reputation, location. The landmarks of a "good match" have been relocated. A modern marriage must be adequate, and adequacy is defined as companionship and successful competition in profession or business. The woman is most highly valued for her performance, and the man for his use of possessions. With the future set for equality, marriage will be a friendly sharing of both.

Self-possessed Sharing

Older assumptions of marriage are being questioned because one partner was totally possessed by the other. Women felt that they surrendered everything and were not satisfied with their returns by modern value standards. One of the new phenomena of marriage counseling is, therefore, the young matron who married young, gained her education or job skills over a period of years, and now "wants out." Having obtained social or economic equality, the over-under basis of her marriage is unsatisfying and she sees no opportunity for equality with this husband.

Modern marriage requires mutual sharing to the extent that equals enjoy each other, and no more. This does not rule out generosity and compassion when our companion is defeated, distressed, disabled. But our sharing will be understood as a voluntary act like that which we would appreciate from a person of equal status. It is not a requirement of society in which the weak are tied to the strong or the noble show mercy to the servant. An example of this distinction is the steady move toward equal language and practice in legislation on marriage, family, business transactions, social usage.

The guiding virtue of companionship marriage must be prudence. This is the *application* of faith, hope, and love in specific circumstances. Without some judicious weighing of inner desire against known reality, we will face the same handicaps of friendship as when the industrial revolution began. Until the days of commercialism, the most-valued friendship was imprudent. A friend would ruin himself financially as surety for his friend. Luther and Calvin protested that a man would thereby lose his place as father, husband, and substantial productive citizen. The classic sense of friendship lingered on in traditional societies, such as the antebellum South, but could not endure in competitive, commercial society. Each man did have to look out for himself. There was no extended family, no guild, no class to protect his friendly imprudence.

In a commercial society, married life is a controlled friendship. We are continually sharing with another but without total surrender. We still possess individuality, which makes friendship endure. Without the cultivation of our own talents, we would not have the attraction that is basic to true comradeship. Instead of total sharing, or complete surrender, the goal of modern marriage is both sowing and reaping, gathering and scattering. We give of ourselves to a partner but we also cultivate in ourselves the virtues that the other admires in us. Unless the circumstances are unusual, we are only committing half of ourselves.

Some Building Principles

Controlled sharing will sound like "half a marriage," or none at all to traditionalists. Many middle-aged people have lived "half" a marriage, but it has been within the shell of conventional matrimony. On the outside it looks like total commitment. All necessary actions are done together. But within, the partner lives for himself, or for his relatives, or for any other interests. He or she is most unwilling for the screen of custom to be rolled up. Their actual relationships must not be revealed. In the next chapter we will review a typical case of conventional marriage, in which each partner was gradually reduced to the status of a puppet. Respectability pulled the wife, and economics the husband. As their intimate relationships decreased, the strings of convention were strengthened. From this disguised study of Mr. and Mrs. Gaston we will derive one working principle for the renewal of marriage: *Cut convention while you can.*

This principle does not imply a disregard for our personal history or social background. We cut the bonds of outdated custom in order that we may enjoy the real pleasures of our past. A strong marriage is built upon clean memories. We can only dare to be different today if we have reliable assurances from previous tests of friendship. Loyalty leads to adventure. We can "be free" if we know the ground on which we stand. So, to enjoy marriage today, cash in on your old accounts. *Refresh yourself with faithful memories.* This is our second principle. It is not always perfected, and in Chapter 3 we will consider ways to develop inner confidence that is based on tested friendship.

If we like what we remember about ourselves and each other, sharing in marriage will be satisfying. But it will not be an end in itself. We share to grow together—and separately. "Total surrender," so popular in sentimental tunes, destroys marriage in the modern world. Adequate and realistic adjustment to our society will require both an openness to new assumptions about matrimony and a reservation of the self from exploitation. Neither man nor woman has the protections of previous generations: dowry, code of honor, family loyalty, community censure. Because we are more "on our own" we cannot completely own or be owned by anyone. This is the third principle: *Share without surrender.*

The principle violates the basic teaching and practice of the human potential movement: in T-groups and sensitivity laboratories we are urged toward instant intimacy. We are to tell and show everything about ourselves. At least this is the popular assumption, the public announcement about "growth groups." As we'll see in Chapter 5, there is much to learn from the human potential movement, but with the restraint of hope. Those who hope for tomorrow don't have to grasp every experience today. We can save something for the future, including a part of ourselves.

Growth groups are an aid to couples who don't know their emotions, who are too inhibited to feel, or too mixed up to interpret their hopes and fears. They find a way to interpret their dreams, but all dreams do not come true in a day. Only in the fairyland of an encounter marathon do we "realize" everything in a moment of time.

For survival in a changing world, we must have hope and a self-awareness that relates dream to reality. This is a process of time and fellowship. A couple learn together over the years the true meaning of their fantasies, the best way to guide hope toward a home. This is one reason for liking the person you love; living together in trust and honesty will show you who you are in the light of what you thought you would be. You will also learn from the members of your immediate family the inner selves of people who are not quite like you. This is wisdom, the growing reward of an open marriage.

The *interpretation of your dreams* is a fourth growth factor in modern marriage. It implies that there is more to come. Even the most immediate of impulses, such as sex, can have a future. In fact, sex must be enjoyed for tomorrow if it is going to survive today. There is no future for swingers. Instant gratification is their only reward. The paperback sex books and their subjects have this in common; they pass the idle moments of life for us when we have nothing meaningful to do.

The time or tense of sex determines its value for marriage. Sex for yesterday is homosexuality, fetishism, voyeurism, a myriad list of labels for neurotic behavior that is continually seeking symbolic gratification of some childhood hang-up. Sex for today is impulse gratification without faith or hope. Why delay gratification when we know of no future reward? Sex for tomorrow is joy in another who will increase the significance of this emotion with an enduring love, an expectation of children, a public commitment of devotion. There will still be this and more tomorrow. The compulsive search for the right technique and for release today is supplanted by anticipation of what each has grown to expect in the other, which is a growing ability to respond together. Those who work with patience at the art of love are rewarded for many years. So if you really like loving, *enjoy sex for tomorrow*. That's principle number five.

But tomorrow may never come. Disease may decrease erotic desire. Disaster may bring depression and chronic anxiety. Death may be only a heartbeat away.

These are not "likable" thoughts, but we will like each other more if we look at them together. Mutual respect grows out of realistic and sensible decisions in a crisis, out of hope despite despair, out of work together when misfortune has torn down some dreams.

This kind of maturity is missing in some modern marriage manuals. There is nothing about sickness, death, or misfortune in Nena and George O'Neill's popular book, *Open Marriage.* I suspect that this dark part of life is too much for some who want out of family life at age thirty-five or forty-five. In *Life*'s feature story of a "dropout wife," Wanda Adams told of two miscarriages, a stillbirth, and the premature birth of Christopher, who had a 70 percent hearing loss. She accepted it all then as a part of "woman's lot." But that was not enough to bear his temper tantrums on top of the usual frustrations of a middle-aged mother with three children. Women—and men—need more profound explanations of the limitations of life and deeper resources than they find in themselves to endure inexplicable tragedy. If we let the thought of death into our living today, we will not run scared from the future or hide the reality of present disabilities.

There is room for these limitations in conventional marriage, especially in those classes which have borne deprivation and frustration for generations. In a nationwide survey for the Joint Commission on Illness and Health, Dr. Gurin found the more-educated respondents to be more sensitive to both the positive and the negative aspects of marriage. Less-educated persons endured frustration with little reflection on their lot.[11]

The people who read this book are on the educational level with highest expectations and demands from marriage. But I fear that we are asking for too much. As Mervyn Cadwallader noted in "Marriage as a

Wretched Institution," there is no history of the marriage institution as a provider of friendship, erotic experience, personal fulfillment, romance, continuous lay psychotherapy, and recreation. "The Western European family was not designed to carry a lifelong load of highly emotional romantic freight." [12]

Even those couples with exceptional resources are strained to meet the idealistic heights of interpersonal fulfillment. In his study of the affluent, John Cuber found that the most vulnerable marriages are those which stress sharing and intimate emotional attachments. The great expectations become grounds for divorce.[13]

Friendship does not carry this pressure to meet all the needs of another person. It is a more relaxed relationship because of mutual enjoyment between adequate people. There is less strain to fill up another with insight, comfort, pleasure, solace, guidance. We don't have to be everything to a mature companion.

In a friendship marriage we live for less. Our expectations are not so idealistic as in romantic marriage, our demands not so great as the therapeutic ideal of upper-class matrimony. This is the sixth principle: *Like each other more by living together with fewer emotional requirements.* Let limitations and failure be a part of marriage.

Of course, limitations and failures can be misinterpreted. Idealistic couples may think that any unhappiness is a sign that their relationship is ruined. Inexperience may be labeled as lack of love or selfishness or thoughtlessness. At such times we must lift up another principle: *Let love have its seasons.* Marriage is a process, with heights of romance at one time and strains of responsibility at another. Freedom and responsibility, eros and agape, delight in another and sober reflection on imperfections will rise and fall with the passing of years. All cannot be experienced in the first year; the feelings experienced in a twenty-year-old marriage should not be compared with those of a honeymoon.

Marriage that lives with the seasons of life will have a place for growth that is missing in romantic love. We always expect the first flush of passion in our idealism of romance. In some sense it is always true that love is young, for over the years we carry a sense of tenderness for every expression of affection. But passion must be tempered with patience and the height of desire moderated to middle-aged anticipation of leisure in lovemaking.

The seasons of life mean death and rebirth of ideals. Illness, misfortune, or heavy responsibility reveal more of us than was visible during the honeymoon period. In time we discover how each is molded separately by the events of marriage. If we can bear to see this individuality, our marriage will endure. If we expect more romance and togetherness, the strain may be too great.

Adaptation to changing circumstances is a mark of a mature marriage. The concept of friendship goes beyond this to accept aging and idiosyncracies. We don't require friends to be eternally young in physique or always pleasing in characteristics. If we translate this to married love, we would like our partner at every stage of life and accept the changes of age and events as an awareness of individuality. We are more different as we mature, but we can become mature enough to live with the differences.

2

Cut Convention if You Can

The principles of companionship marriage are for people who can grow. They provide mutual fulfillment for an adequate couple. The goal is enhancement of individuality and mutual respect between people in love.

But what if one or both persons are inadequate? Then a traditional marriage may be appropriate. Convention may be substituted for competence when the mates are unequal. Rigid roles are played to cover inadequacy and to control hostility. Outward conformity masks inward despair.

What happens to people who cannot cut convention? They die a little bit at a time. On some occasions they are aware that the core of their being has decayed, but they may not wish to give up the shell of social security that now encases their hollow self.

This was the struggle of Mrs. Gaston. She was a middle-aged woman who never intended any unhappiness for herself or her family. She cannot understand the reluctance of her grown children to come home. She vaguely hints that her husband does not respect her.

"Why can't I be happy like other people?" asked Mrs. Gaston of her pastor. "I've tried to do right. Perhaps I've been too strict with the children, but I always wanted the best for them and I couldn't bear to think that they would be criticized by others. They are so dear to me. But they were so unruly and stubborn. Now they pay no attention to me. I've tried the best I know how. But all they say is that I was all wrapped up in myself."

MR. ROGOW: Did they specify the reason for that accusation?

MRS. GASTON: Well, my daughter did tell me one time, when she came home from college—that seems a long time ago—that I put more store in other peoples' opinion of me than I did in their happiness. I said I could never accept that. I was only trying to protect them from criticism. They have no idea of the way people talk in this town. It would kill me for someone to speak ill of them.

MR. ROGOW: You do seem to be very concerned about what other people think—perhaps what they think of you as a mother.

MRS. GASTON: Well, I should hope so! What does a woman have besides her reputation? That's what I was taught. Of course, my children grew up under other influences. Their friends stayed out late at night, and I don't guess that their parents cared very much. But I wanted the parents to know that I cared about my children and what happened to them. But it didn't seem to make any impression on them.

MR. ROGOW: I believe you said their impression was that you were selfish, or something like that.

MRS. GASTON: That's what *they* say. But I never bought a thing for myself. I shopped continually for them. George [the oldest son] never made a bed in his life! Nellie was no better. She just wanted to run around with her friends after school. Now that she's married and has that dear sweet AnnaBelle, she said she isn't going to yell at her daughter the way I yelled at her. Well, I just couldn't help it sometimes. They were so aggravating.

MR. ROGOW: It sounds as though each member of your family has gone his own independent way. You weren't able to get the children to do as you wanted them to do.

MRS. GASTON: Lord, it was not for *me*. I was only thinking of them. I know a few things about the world and how people have to get along. I was taught how to get along. If I hadn't had those contacts in college, we would never have had the friends we have today or move in the circles we do. My children have been brought up with the best associations possible. My father wanted that for each of us girls and I have seen to it that my girls have better than I had. Of course, I couldn't do much about the crowd they ran with, that was just impossible. They paid no attention to me.

MR. ROGOW: Mrs. Gaston, I'm not quite sure as to why you have come to see me today.

MRS. GASTON: I have something to cheer you up. People listen to your sermons. At least I listened to the one last Sunday. You quoted some authority who said that a woman's personhood could be smothered in motherhood—

MR. ROGOW: Oh, yes, oh, yes. I was talking about women's liberation. I was agreeing with them that a woman needs a life of her own. Now, of course, I was not trying to say that you could just do anything you wanted to do. I know we have to keep our moral standards.

MRS. GASTON: Well, I got to thinking about that part on motherhood. Clarke [Mr. Gaston] hit me with something like that when we were on vacation last month. We were coming back from the lake and he said something about enjoying things like they used to be. When I asked what he meant, he said that I showed some interest in him and in doing things. He said that in the past I've been all wrapped up in the children and never talked to him about anything but them. In fact, I have the feeling that he is thinking of asking for a divorce. I can read him like a book.

MR. ROGOW: What makes you so sure about that?

MRS. GASTON: Whenever he wants to lead up to something, he gives examples of other people. Then finally he springs his own idea on me. So, for a couple of months he has been talking about friends and acquaintances who are getting divorces. He has been talking about the specifics like who got the house and who had to pay how much money. Well, while we were up at the lake, he made some remark like, "I think I would like to keep the house here at the lake and let you have the one in town, if something were to happen to us like it did Jake and Lela." Those two had just finished a property settlement. Oh, I know just what is going through his mind.

MR. ROGOW: And what is going through your mind?

MRS. GASTON: I'll take him for every cent he has. He'll not ruin my reputation without it costing him something. I built up a good name for myself in this town, and my family means something. If he can't keep up appearances for the sake of the children and myself, then I'll drain him. He'll never get away with this.

MR. ROGOW: You're really going to get him.

MRS. GASTON: Right. When he gets around to telling me what's on his mind, I'm going to nail him to the wall.

MR. ROGOW: Well, you were saying something about my sermon. In some way it prompted you to come and talk.

MRS. GASTON: Yes! You know, that part about the puppet. (*Looks inquiringly at the minister.*)

MR. ROGOW: Oh, you mean that quote from C. S. Lewis about the man on a chain? Oh, yes, I remember that from seminary days. The man started out with a puppet on a chain, kind of like a monkey. Then the puppet began to talk for the man and grew larger. His wife would talk to the man, but the puppet would answer. Finally the puppet was a giant and the man was a pygmy. Then the woman would have to kneel down to get close to the man and talk to him. She refused to talk to the puppet.

MRS. GASTON: Yes, well I'm not quite sure that I agree with this man that you quoted. I mean, there are some things in life that you have to do. Sometimes you're not appreciated. People make accusations against you like Clarke did. I don't know if he read what you read or not, but now he's telling me that I haven't been an interesting wife. He doesn't seem to consider what I have done for the children. And they don't appreciate what I have done, so why shouldn't I be unhappy?

MR. ROGOW: I must say that I'm confused right now.

You talk about being unhappy, but seem quite certain of yourself and the things that you have done. May I have a little time to think about this? Would Clarke be willing to talk with me? I don't know if this is a concern to him right now or not.

MRS. GASTON: Well, I think that Clarke would probably talk to you sooner or later anyway, since he has that divorce in his mind. I just want it to be private, that's all.

On the following Saturday, when Mr. Rogow took his children out to the lake, he saw Mr. Gaston working alone on his boat at the family dock. Mr. Rogow walked over and sat down on the pier.

MR. GASTON: Well, hello, preacher. I'm glad to see that you're getting out for a little fun once in a while. Man, do I enjoy getting out here on this boat. It's really great, I wouldn't trade anything for this cottage. Of course, I had to sell Maude [Mrs. Gaston] on the idea. When she saw it would be a good thing for the kids, she went along with it.

MR. ROGOW: Well, it sure is fun to be out here, I'm sure. I guess you will want to keep the cottage?

MR. GASTON: Oh? I guess Maude has been in to talk with you, right? (*Pastor nods.*) So, I'm getting ready to propose a settlement with her. It has taken me a little time to figure out just how to get out of this marriage without it costing me too much.

MR. ROGOW: How come you want out?

MR. GASTON: Because I don't have a wife anymore. I haven't had one in ten or fifteen years. She doesn't respond to my attention to her, she doesn't show any interest in things we used to do, she doesn't think about anything but how the children are doing and how she is going to look good around town.

MR. ROGOW: Those are strong words.

MR. GASTON: O.K., I guess they are. Well, let me give you an example. We came up here to the lake for a couple of days. I thought it was real nice. Just the two of us. We sat out on the porch and watched the sun set. She didn't see a d—— thing. I reached over and put my arm around her and began to make love to her. She didn't move. Then she suddenly said, "Clarke, don't you think that Nellie and AnnaBelle would like to come up here this weekend. I'd have to stay close to the baby so she doesn't get too close to the lake. Why don't we call and ask them if they would like to do that?" Well, I guess that's a good thing to think about and I guess we should do it. But that was the end of making love! She just got up and said that she would make some dessert for us. I don't need dessert!

MR. ROGOW: You need love.

MR. GASTON: Oh, well, we do pretty well once or twice a month. And then when we go to some movie where there is romance she gets real soft and eager. Then she's like she was when we were first married. Or sometimes the women in the bridge club will get to talking about their husbands and she will come home and tell me how she bragged on me as a good man. Sometimes she wants sex then. But then sometimes she just talks about me as one of her accomplishments and never responds when I say thanks for the good word or try to love her.

MR. ROGOW: You don't think that she is responding to you as a person.

MR. GASTON: Oh, boy! That's a phrase I learned in

the management course last year. Well, I guess it does work. You hit on the thing that used to bother me a great deal. I mean, I used to be quite sentimental; sometimes when she had hurt me I'd go down in the basement and mope around with the shop tools for hours.

MR. ROGOW: So it really did hurt.

MR. GASTON: Sure, sure. But I got a thing figured out that way. That is, she doesn't really mean anything personal by the way she treats me. You know, she isn't really trying to hurt me or anything like that. Well, sometimes she might get mad and really jab me, but most of the time she would hurt me by ignoring me or turning away when I tried to show her some affection or tell her something that I was feeling. Anyway, I figure now that she doesn't go for that kind of thing. Her mother and father never had much of a relationship. He was a good provider and she was—well, I guess I shouldn't talk about the in-laws. Anyway, nothing was ever very warm in her home and she just doesn't think about that now that she doesn't have the children to fuss over.

MR. ROGOW: I don't quite get all of this. You talked a while ago about the way she was when you were first married. It seemed to be a very warm relationship, and now—

MR. GASTON: Yeah, yeah. That's what confused me for a long time. She was a very happy and warm person when we were first married. But when the children came, she transferred all the attention to them. I guess she just settled down then to the model from her own family and—well, I guess she's also influenced by those people she runs with. She set her mind to build a respectable family and a good reputation for herself and the children so that's what she has done. So long as I help to keep things up to her standards she lets me lead a peaceful life. But there is just nothing in it like there was when we were first married. Well, I must say— (*Telephone rings in cottage.*) Excuse me. (*Answers telephone.*) O.K., we'll do that now . . . Excuse me, preacher, but there are some people that I have to see now. It's been real good for you to come by and I hope that you'll stay with Maude when the time comes for us to separate. Well, good-by for now. I'll see you again.

The Puppet That Grew

Conventional roles have filled up the hollow place where affection was once to be found in the soul of Mrs. Gaston. There isn't much in life for her beyond her social activities. In conversations with club members she must speak about her husband and children as accomplishments. If she can brag about them, her status is increased. If they fail her in some way, she is infuriated. They are then a cause of embarrassment to her.

Mrs. Gaston is like her pastor's illustration of the puppet that grew. Convention has become so strong that she has no control over her own feelings. In fact, she is now unaware of the sense of romance and the mutual respect that were once possibilities in her marriage.

This is the kind of closed marriage that young people have seen with some parents. It has led to the great popularity of books and lectures on open and free relationships. Youth do not want to enter an institution that would drain away life and reduce people to puppets on a string.

When we look at this kind of marriage, our usual impulse is to condemn the culture or the institution of marriage itself. But I think that this is a superficial judgment. We should balance our condemnation of culture with an awareness of Mrs. Gaston's personal inadequacy. Convention is her crutch. She has used the shibboleths of society to maintain herself. What else could she do? *If* she had known an understanding pastor, physician, or marriage counselor in early days, she might have accepted the risk of individuality and of open relationships with her husband and her children. But even if this possibility had existed, how much progress would she have made?

The plight of the Gastons is a warning against "social" marriage. But it is also a lesson in the way that social roles maintain those who do not have satisfying relationships with a partner.

Relief Without Reform

What happens to a marriage that is swallowed up in convention? In this case, Mr. Gaston would like to get out. Divorce is becoming a realistic alternative for more people in middle age.

But sometimes the cost is too great. Mr. Gaston talked on other occasions with his pastor about what he would have to give up if he asked for a divorce. At the present time, he cannot pay back the money that his wife has invested in his business. She would demand this as part of the divorce settlement, and he would be financially ruined. He seemed to obtain some

est, Mrs. Gaston prefers her bridge partners and Mr. Gaston prefers his boat on the lake. Neither wants to be with the other for companionship. At one time Mr. Gaston thought that he would get some value out of the relationship by making love to his wife, but she soon frustrated that hope and now is relieved to find that his heart attack has made him less demanding.

How can we cut the strings of convention early enough in the relationship to prevent the tragic puppet show of the Gastons? One answer is to stress the inner qualities of faith, hope, and love. The development of strong character is an antidote to overbearing demands for social conformity. Those who are sure of themselves will not need continual reassurance from relatives or bridge partners. They will find satisfaction with each other, without having to act as though they did everything together. There will be a sharing of dreams and disappointments, the building up of hope, and the growth of character through steadfastness in both temptation and disappointment.

These are the qualities of an equalitarian marriage that will allow men and women to either take or leave the conventions of their culture. If a custom cradles some truth in which they believe, it should be respected. But as social arbiters press for some conformity that is not true to the marriage relationship, the couple can remind their anxious friends that the customs of marriage are changing. The traditional ways may benefit some, but there are also some new paths to self-acceptance after a wedding ceremony. In the following chapters we will follow three guideposts to more intimate relationships in an equalitarian marriage: faith, hope, and love. These are the inner virtues of character that are nurtured in a trusted friendship.

3

Look Back with Faith

We cut the bonds of outdated customs in order that we may enjoy the real pleasures of our past. A weak marriage may need the bonds of convention to hold it together; a strong marriage is built on clean memories that do not restrict us in the present.

To build a marriage on friendship, refresh your memory. Recall what you have promised in the past and perform it. This is the foundation of competence between intimate partners.

Steadfastness is of special value in a modern society of instant gratification. It is easy to forget the past in the world that lives only for today. The caricature of modern marriage is presented in one television comedy after another. Husband or wife become expert manipulators. Their actions are concealed for the sake of present convenience, their promises are reinterpreted, their circumstances change with bewildering rapidity. In these comedies husband, wife, or some close friend is the "straight" person who is always trying to reconcile the promises of yesterday with the peculiar events of the present.

The basic problem in instant gratification is a lack of faithfulness. The partner is not true to anything but his own impulses; nothing can be planned with confidence. The past is disregarded, so the future is uncertain. A person without roots may bluff his way through a change of plans without any reference to his new direction. If he is reminded of a commitment, he may pretend that he "forgot." Or he may shrug his shoulders and say that he changed his mind. Then he expects the partner to quickly adapt to altered circumstances. If there is hesitation, the disappointed partner is accused of being slow, square, uninterested in fulfillment "now."

The New Demand for Character

Our society has magnified instant gratification and diminished approval for a delay of personal satisfactions. This change of values is especially disastrous in a time when myriad satisfactions are more available than at any previous time in our history. The market for the youth culture has expanded to the place where clothing stores, excursion trips, apartment complexes, and business advertisements are built around this new style of life. So much is offered immediately that young people wonder why anything should be delayed until tomorrow. Everything seems to be available now. There are so many good choices that no one is made to feel bad if he swiftly changes courses, jobs, apartments, or partners. There are so many alternatives that it is difficult to set any priorities.

At the same time, the older channels of social development have been neglected. Curfew hours in college dormitories have been lifted. Chaperons and housemothers are disappearing. There are no watchful eyes over the convention. The couple may conform to company expectations as the ambitious man may rise in prominence but they also can find a select group of friends who do not care how they act at a party, as long as no one tells.

Social ostracism was once a controlling force over shallow commitment. The person who lacked roots was held in line by gossip and stern glances. There were definite penalties for impulsive gratification. If a husband or wife did not remember his pledges, there were always parents, grandparents, uncles, aunts, and older siblings to remind them. In the extended family of a nineteenth-century small town, people knew what others were doing and made it their business to keep friends and relatives on a steady schedule through courtship, marriage, parenthood, and respectable old age.

The restraints of the past are inoperative in many areas of modern society. Yet the need for some control of superficial commitment and impulsive change of direction has become an acute problem in marriage. How shall the problem be solved? Three general solutions are possible. One is to return to the old ways and steady the unstable through community pressure. This is a method which is still used in settled communities and retains some influence with the other-directed couple in the upper middle classes. But society is too mobile for continual checks on those who wander and moral values are too varied for any universal application of penalties through social disapproval. If a person does not feel that he is well accepted in one group, he moves to another.

A second remedy is to obliterate memory and thus reduce anxiety over varying decisions. The popular use of drugs has anesthetized many to the results of their own rootlessness. Loss of contact with the past does not make any difference when you can sleep through the present. In addition to drugs, there is an insistent emphasis of the "now" culture upon the full expansion of human potential in every moment of time. This is considered therapeutic justification for freedom from previous restraints. People are urged to break with past inhibitions and to feel better by doing what comes naturally in this moment of time. A variety of new therapies have been devised to assist people to instant awareness and action.

This commitment to immediate emotion would be valuable if it were combined with an awareness of the past and an affirmation of the goals in life. But an extraction of feeling can be very unfaithful to the long-term development of character. After a weekend marathon, the participant may have inappropriate expectations of family, friends, and work associates. They may have no intense interest in why the person is angry at this moment of time and in when he is aware of bodily impulses that were formerly suppressed. The group that supported his intense awareness at the retreat center have now scattered. He is back at the old job with people who expect him to produce or he may be at home with a family who have needs of their own.

Do these difficulties mean that self-awareness should be inhibited? No, my quarrel is with the limited vision of sensitivity training. People are led to concentrate so much upon the present that they are not fully aware of what they have been in relation to their present and future desires. Unless the past can be brought into the present, the future will be fragmented. Several training groups have become aware of this danger and have deliberately "socialized" their members before returning them to the community. A typical question might be, "You have told us of some of your frustrations with your present, but how would you talk about this with your boss?" or "You certainly have some strong needs for affection from other people, and now you must consider how that can be expressed in your family. Will they be able to respond?" Most especially, the past is related to the present in therapy groups for alcoholics and drug abusers. One of the most common queries is: "These are some excellent promises that you make now, but in what way is your attitude different today than it was three weeks ago when you were in the clinic?" or, "You ask us to believe you now, but how are you going to show more faithful behavior than we have seen in the past?"

Foundation Stones for Marriage

We can bear to be different today only if we have reliable assurance from previous tests of friendship. When there is some confidence from performance in the past, we can be assured of loyalty in the present. This is a third solution to the problem of a rootless society. We can move about securely in changing circumstances when we really know who we are and how we have been committed. Faithful memories from the past give us freedom from both guilt and insecurity in the present.

I am not recommending a morbid introspection in which a person stops to consider every comparison between present opportunities and previous choices. I am suggesting that memory is a messenger of faith and faithlessness. It is a valuable interpreter of what is happening now because there are readings from the past. For example, a wife may remark to a counselor that her husband is more attentive to the children now that they are teen-agers. She sees new hope for the family as she contrasts his previous indifference to his present awakening as a father who has interesting children. Or a husband may measure his moods of this year against those of previous years and conclude that he is better able to stand the stress of life with a neurotic wife. As one man told me: "I thought when I came to see you that I couldn't stand any more. But now that you have asked me some questions, I have convinced myself that I don't go to pieces so easily as I used to when she pulls one of her fancy moods. I really must be getting better!"

Memory is essential to the measurement of progress or decay in any relationship. We look for progress in love or decay in hate.

Strong love depends on clean memories. We are renewed by pleasure from the past. We are literally living on the dividends of previous actions and attitudes. A wife may wait patiently through the debilitating illness of her husband because she can sit by his side and remember the happy times when they sat together under more healthy circumstances. If he begins to recover, she can smile and remind him that he is now "as he used to be." Satisfactions from the past give her patience in the present.

Likewise, a husband's thoughts from his storehouse

of memory will often keep him faithful in the crucial years after thirty-five when middle-class men often begin to wander. As he considers some fleeting pleasure for the moment, he may ask himself: "Should I destroy all that I have built up over these years and cloud my conscience with guilt?" Conscience is a sensitive repository of the past. It is a continual reminder of what we have been. It may bring some reality to the middle-aged man who thinks that he will now return to escapades that he missed as a youth. What will keep him from sin? It may be the sight of a young family, which reminds him of the trusting of his own children in their early days or the shared experiences with his wife when life was more difficult and uncertain. Now that he is older and wiser, he can enjoy the fruits of that kind of living. He can reap the rewards of righteousness rather than seek to sow some overripe oats.

Respect for the past is important for many reasons in marriage. The most obvious reason is an awareness of the causes for the enhancement or inhibitions of love in the present. Another is the lesson from people who have had more experience than we have had. We see now the results of previous experiences in their life. This helps us to plan our own future. We may delay the gratification of some present impulse on behalf of some future peace and satisfaction. Delayed gratification is built on an assurance that time is on the side of those who plan ahead. This is a difficult thing to learn for impulsive people. They believe that the only gratification is immediate. They must seize what pleasure they can *now*. A wife may spend without reason because she does not really believe that she and her husband will accumulate better things in the future. A husband may continue to "fly off the handle" despite damages to his family, because he cannot really see how controlling his temper will help.

Marriage counseling is in part an investigation of the past and in part a building of that past into the present. We investigate what has happened and we also teach some impulsive people that better things will happen if they can begin to think ahead. We remind them that revival of behavior modification is an attempt to put time into our relationships. We set goals for twenty-four hours or more. Then we pledge ourselves to keep certain promises to each other during that period of time. Soon we are rewarded or punished for what happened during that space of time. We learn by degrees to get satisfaction.

I think that behavior modification works best for marriages so broken that mechanical procedures are necessary. There is no warm interpersonal relationship on which some people can restore their home. But they can go through certain motions that break the vicious cycle of frustration. He can say what would please him for today and what he is willing to do to please her. There may be some restraint on angry words and hateful behavior. It is not the final solution but it is a beginning. We cannot persuade these people to talk about their long-term attitudes unless we can reduce some of the tension and hopelessness that is in their homes.

In contrast, insight therapy is more useful when people have more control of themselves. They can talk and presumably they can act on the basis of what they say. Our problem with them is to unblock attitudes, to reset relationships.

Much of marriage counseling is a cleaning operation.

It is a plunge through the cake of indifference that protects injured persons from each other. It is an investigation of the hate that has distorted pleasure and erased happy memories.

One young man faced his past in the course of premarital counseling. Mr. Carl, who was twenty-eight years old, had just told one reason for resentment against his mother. She had controlled everything as long as he could remember. When he wanted to attend parties as a teen-ager, his mother would forbid him by saying that the people were not good enough for him. She prevented his father from giving him money for clothing or entertainment when the son was in college. The mother had never met a girl or a boy who really came up to her expectations.

Mr. Carl was now locked in rage against his mother. He wanted to marry a girl whom he would respect, but he was continually frightened by those who had an independent spirit. They might control him as had his mother. Now he was engaged to a girl who balanced an independent spirit with a willingness to let him take the lead in some things. "But," he said, "I just have so much resentment against any woman who tries to tell me what to do. I just cannot make up my mind to get married. It might be just like it was for my parents."

I wanted to know if he was going to continue his rage for a lifetime. Now that he had explored the reasons for resentment, was he going to use this as an excuse for isolation from others? He could not continue to hold other people responsible for what his mother had done to him. Now was the time for him to take some responsibility for himself. How was he going to act on the basis of what he knew?

Mr. Carl had maintained for a long time that his mother would never change. This justified a lack of change in the son. But now he began to think of himself as something different from a thwarted adolescent. He was being treated by others as a man in his own right. His mother might never change, but he could. One evidence of that change would be an alteration in his attitude toward her. Instead of viewing her as the all-powerful parent, he could now see why she needed so much to control those who were close to her. Once he began to see the world in a different way from his mother, she lost some of her power over him.

When we try to clean up memories, we often talk about forgiveness. Faith will not be bright and strong if it is clouded by resentment. But our speeches about forgiveness will not be effective unless we see the hurt of the past in the light of present hope. We might remind ourselves that no one forgives the same person twice. Both of us have changed since the initial hurt. Mr. Carl could not forgive his mother when he was an adolescent because he was too vulnerable. But now that he is a man with mature and respected relationships, he can afford forgiveness. That is, he can receive the gift that God is ready to give him. Before this it was much too threatening; it would have carried an obligation of strength and maturity that he could not fulfill.

Forgiveness is both a recognition that we have changed and a willingness to change. It is a sign that we are not going to stay with the same stale hate. The stakes of life are too great for us to entrench ourselves in regrets from the past.

What is at stake? For most people, it is a question

of brightness versus dullness. I find that a faithless middle-class marriage is more dull than destructive. The people have enough control to keep up appearances in the community and before the children. They usually live in houses that are big enough for separate bedrooms and two televisions. The man has his telephone and briefcase in the evening, or travel and conventions. The couple live on together, but the man and wife have less and less to like in each other.

The Fruits of Faith

The exercise of memory is a search for self-identity. We are shaped by the significant experiences of the past. If certain people have been faithful to us, then we have faith in ourselves. We believe that there is some success in life for us because of patient teaching by trial and error and encouragement to improve the craftsmanship of living. And, as we are successful in one or more adventures, we become more assured and skillful to attempt the next task. Success ensures success. We become likable because others like us.

We have great need of this confidence for the major engagements of life. Unless we have some sureness about ourselves, we are not going to risk openness in courtship, engagement, marriage, friendships, or professional relationships. Each of these crucial experiences of life is an adventure of faith in other people and in ourselves.

Along with these crucial ventures of normal living there are the crises of misfortune, illness, evil, and miscalculation. As the writer of the Letter to the Hebrews puts it, we have "need of endurance, for life is a hard struggle with sufferings."

The Biblical writer was referring primarily to the struggles of Christians in a non-Christian world. I believe that his insights can also be applied to all human relationships. The author gives a general admonition that we are to avoid the "root of bitterness" that springs up and "causes trouble." Instead, we are to strive for peace with all men. (Heb. 12:12–15.)

What are the characteristics of this faithful life that will root out bitterness and give us peace? I find at least six lessons in the tenth, eleventh, and twelfth chapters of the Letter to the Hebrews.

First, there is an open admission that conflict in life is inevitable. We are to "recall the former days" of hard struggle. I wish that a young husband of my acquaintance could apply this verse to himself. He acts like one who has attained perfection through denial of self. He came to me with a request that I help him understand his wife better. When I saw them together, she would admit to many conflicts, but his only complaint was that he did not have enough understanding of her. Every inquiry I made of his background was met with denial of problems. He would admit that there had been some difficulties in his family, but none of that touched him now. It took several interviews for him to admit that he was "tied up in knots" and had been sent by his family physician to see me. It will be difficult for him to admit very much. His wife expects him to be a very adequate person. If he admits to any failing, what will she think of him? He has no wish to be "publicly exposed to abuse." Perhaps when she learns to have compassion on him, he may be able to talk about the sufferings that he endures.

For the present, there is inequality in this marriage.

He removes himself from the normal struggles of mankind. What kind of a friend can that be?

A second aspect of faith is "assurance of things hoped for." A list of activities by the heroes of faith are given in the eleventh chapter of Hebrews. In psychological terms we would describe this as goal-directed behavior.

In family life we would see this goal-directed behavior as a willingness to keep on living at a high level despite the temptations of hate and hopelessness. If one person in a family can keep this kind of faith, then that person, at least, will be saved—and probably some others as well. It may be a mother, a father, or a child. It is a saving grace that is the result of some very adequate resources poured into the life of this person over a period of years. Sometimes it is the result of a happy childhood that prevents a husband or wife from ever responding in kind to bitterness, jealousy, hopelessness, or anxiety. The person simply was not raised to respond in this way.

The supposed invulnerability of an adequate person will be very irritating to a spouse. This was a problem for Mr. and Mrs. Park who had been married for more than ten years. Mrs. Park suffered from periodic depression. As she was going into despondency or coming out of it, she was exceedingly critical of her family. Mr. Park would not respond in kind. Instead, he would offer many reassurances that she would soon feel better. This further enraged his wife. As she told her psychiatrist, her husband always had a big healthy smile. He never seemed to understand what other people were going through.

Mr. Park took some time with his therapist to understand himself and his wife. After several interviews he began to talk about his own background. He had always been well accepted by his family and had always been successful in everything that he had attempted. Though he had known people in his business who gave way to despair and self-doubt, his wife was the only person close to him who had ever shown these feelings. Gradually he began to realize that his own background was exceptional. Not many people had been as fortunate as he had been. Many more people lived now with a background like that of his wife. If he could begin to understand her better, then he might be able to work better with some of his employees, who now withdrew from him when he made demands on them.

If Mr. Park can temper his confidence with compassion, he will be a source of faith to his wife and also to his children. He has already shown a good deal of understanding by asking his wife if she wants to move into a new home, leaving the decisions about room locations and decorations to her. This is the first time that he has really allowed her to set her own pace and make her own decisions. Now they begin to relate as equals. He respects her as he would a good friend. The old dominance and protectiveness is diminishing.

A part of the therapy with Mr. Park is an illustration of the third lesson from Hebrews. This is the use of faith as an alternative to hatred and hopelessness. We can show or suggest different ways of coping with anxiety and stress. Mr. Park learned to be factual in dealing with some of his wife's dark spots about ambiguous circumstances. On one occasion she was moody because one of her acquaintances did not recognize her in the drugstore. This seemed to her to be a sure sign that people hated and despised her. They were all hypocrites who played up to her on social occasions in the presence of her husband, but who then ignored her when they saw her alone. The therapist suggested that the husband offer some alternative explanations. Perhaps a person did not recognize her because of preoccupation. Or perhaps the wife was dressed differently. If the date for a party is changed, it may not mean that people do not want her to come. Perhaps there is a sick child in the house or something like that. The husband should admit that the wife's interpretation may sometimes be correct but should continually interpose the possibility that some alternate explanations are possible. There is much evil in the world, but this does not mean that everyone is evil around us all the time. We do not need to make a general catastrophe out of isolated misfortunes.

Mr. Park can accept that very well for himself because he has a general plan for his life that will allow him to accept minor frustrations. He can modify his plans in time of emergency because he is confident of the ultimate success of his decisions. This is another lesson from the writer of Hebrews. The early Christians were able to endure suffering and privation because they were seeking a homeland which is heavenly. The distress of the present time could be endured because they were confident of ultimate success. They were citizens of a kingdom that was beyond the destructive hand of man.

This sense of pilgrimage can be seen in both an approximate and an ultimate sense in marriage. Approximately, it is the setting of goals for the building of a home or a business. This is the case of Mr. Park. Ultimately, it is a recognition that all our striving is partial and will be swallowed up in death and decay. We cannot really control our destiny from day to day. Previous success will increase the possibility that we will succeed now, but there are some devastating crises which are beyond our control. In a companionship marriage, catastrophe can be handled better as an individual problem. That is, we accept our share of responsibility for remaking our existence, but we do not try to take full responsibility for everybody's reaction. Before therapy, Mr. Park would be burdened with anxieties for his whole family. He would not only be worried about the recouping of financial losses but also concerned for the depression of his wife or the anxieties of his children. As the great provider he worried for everybody.

With a more humble acceptance of his own limitations, Mr. Park can worry for himself and let his wife do her own worrying. He can concentrate on the development of mature and stable attitudes within himself. This will enable his wife to set her own direction without being smothered by an overprotective husband. She will take responsibility for her feelings without his help.

This lesson must be balanced against another one from Hebrews, "apart from us they should not be made perfect" (Heb. 11:40). Faith is an appreciation for faithful people from the past. This is the understanding that Mr. Park came to have of himself. He was one of those persons who was not shaken in the present because he had a very secure childhood. The result was more gratitude toward his own family and a willingness to see why other people were not as serene as he was. They did not have the adequacies of his background and could not be expected to smile through misfortunes. Their training had been to become anxious and guilty over every mistake. Mr. Park should not judge them in the light of his own experience. Instead, he should consider the progress that his wife has made from the time that she was under her mother's control until thc present. By that measurement, she is moving toward perfection.

Here again, individuality is the key to more appreciation of a spouse. When Mr. Park can see his wife with her background rather than with his, he can let her develop her own ways of coping with present distress. She in turn will feel less guilty for her occasional moods of despair as she realizes that she must be judged in terms of her own development rather than that of another person.

How do a couple reach the place where they can say how they feel without feeling that they are being judged by the other? How can we realistically lean on each other without being too dependent? These are questions of sharing without submission, which is the topic of our next chapter.

4

Share Without Surrender

The primary aim of marriage in an urban, anonymous world is to provide emotional contact. At least this is the expectation of many couples who are shifted about in a mobile world. It is made more intent by the shrinking of the family to a few persons—mother, father, and one or two children. Grandparents, uncles, aunts, cousins, and childhood friends are either unavailable or undesirable. Every emotional need is to be met by one or two people, who can literally consume each other with their demands. It is the intensity of these demands that has led me to recommend sharing without surrender in marriage. We cannot meet the high emotional expectations of a partner in our anonymous society. No one person can be all things, even to one other person. Just as we have stressed individuality in the previous chapter, so we must consider the boundaries of personality now. A growing person must have some life space between himself and anyone else. There must be some time for him to think his own thoughts, pursue his own interests, keep his own counsel.

This may sound like a withholding of the self from someone we love. In fact, a common complaint in growth groups is a lack of warmth and concern from the marital partner. As we will see in the following case of Mrs. Polk, a marriage can be devastated by the passivity or withdrawal of either partner. When that happens, the deprived husband or wife will become even more insistent that everything be shared. This is one of the reasons for the popularity of growth groups for couples, for the major emphasis of the meeting is upon an open statement of what you feel at any one moment. This is the communication for which many persons hunger in marriage.

I recognize the need for emotional communication and support therapeutic endeavors to reduce isolation. At the same time, I am concerned about the personal identity of each partner. We must be loved for what we are, rather than for what we can pour into the life of another. I believe that the stronger we are as individuals the more able we are to use our personal resources for the benefit of those for whom we care. We can be more helpful and loving because we exercise judgment, control, selective attention. These are attributes of a centered self. They require an awareness of who we are, a sureness of our purpose in life, a belief that we can make a contribution as an individual. This contribution will be most helpful to others when we deliberately decide what we are to share and where. This is different from the popular theme of self-surrender, in which one partner is like a supermarket where his lover may roam freely, consuming whatever he desires.

The cult of love has pushed sharing to such extremes that it becomes exploitation. In a rootless society, where two people have only each other to cling to, this is exhausting. Emotional depletion leads to guilt and recrimination. Each person believes that he should share more and condemns himself for a lack of concern. At the same time, each believes that the other is not "fully giving." The supply-and-demand crisis is intense in the monopolistic dyad. Husband and wife have only each other. They are cut off from the traditional markets of emotional interchange, such as extended family, long-time associates, well-known institutions.

These sources of support were strong when romantic love flourished in Western civilization. The cult of love, from the Middle Ages through Queen Victoria, was based on the assumption that women were constitutionally inferior to men. Men could ask for all their affection because this was all that a woman had to give, except for children. All the man's needs were not met by Victorian women. He was continually advised and sustained by mother, father, brothers, employer, and close friends. The emotional ties that are expected in twentieth-century marriage were usually met in the English upper classes in their clubs—"for men only."

But the private clubs are decreasing, and women expect themselves to be adequate companions for men. This creates a double difficulty. Couples are expecting everything from each other in marriage at the very time that other emotional supports are diminishing. Our current assumption is that a wife can be a lover, adviser, manager, and equal provider with her husband.

If this expectation were based upon a realistic picture of the woman as a person, we would have less depression and anxiety. But we expect all the self-giving of romantic attachments, plus the adequacies of a mature companion, interesting conversationalist, adroit financier, and wise disciplinarian. We are asking the woman to be more than a person because of a picture of love that comes from the time when she was less than a person.

A Friend Has a Lot to Give

Sharing can be sensible when it is based on a realistic appraisal of individual capacities. This has always been our assumption about friendship. There would be less distortion in the modern use of "love" if it were related to some of our traditional expectations of a friend. These expectations can be the foundations for an intimacy in marriage which does not violate individuality. They are also therapeutic resources to restore emotional communication in marriages that have grown stale. One of these marriages was between a couple in their thirties, Mr. and Mrs. Polk.

The first complaint of Mrs. Polk was that her husband did not share equally with her in their marriage. In the first interview she said: "I knew thirty minutes after we were married how he was going to be. As we were turning the corner right after our marriage he saw an old friend from his hometown, got out of the car and talked to him for an hour. In the early days of our marriage I had to do everything that had to be done. He never had any initiative in his job and has never had any advancement. Whatever I have in the way of material things I've purchased for myself. I worked for several years after we were married and then stopped to raise my two children. Now that the girls are in school I have gone back to work because I can't stand to do everything and have nothing in the way of material comforts. I've paid for my car and I am buying many of the furnishings in our home."

But after explaining her self-sufficiency, Mrs. Polk asked: "What can be done when I am like a child? That's the way I am. Anyway, that's what my husband says about me. But I just can't help it. I guess there's nothing I can do about it."

During the rest of that hour, the counselor asked a number of questions that pointed in the direction of new possibilities for Mr. and Mrs. Polk: "Why have you decided that you are a child?" "What are the advantages of remaining this way and what are the disadvantages?" "What would happen if you were to tell your husband some of the things that you are telling me?"

These questions were aimed at the despair of Mrs. Polk. She assumed that she had no choice in her marriage. Was this really true? She appeared to be an aggressive person who could be quite self-sufficient. If this were the case, then her self-affirmation should be connected to her problems of sharing with a husband.

The counselor did not make these connections, but the second interview showed that Mrs. Polk had made some for herself. She said: "I want to take an entirely different approach to things this morning. When I went home Tuesday I just came unglued. I had felt so very self-righteous when I talked to you that morning. It's not easy for me to say this, but I think my own attitude may have something to do with my problem. If so, I want to do something about it. My husband seemed to sense that something was really wrong because he came in and for the first time talked with me about what was wrong. I told him I was just so tired and I didn't want to be taking all this responsibility anymore. I told him all the things that I remember and he said, 'Why do you remember all these things? I can't remember everything like that.' I guess I'm too sensitive and have been expecting too much. People have always said that I was a perfectionist. But anyway I do feel that I need to look at some of these things in myself such as being oversensitive to what happens."

Mrs. Polk is beginning to practice the first principle of friendship in marriage. She is considering her continued relationship with her husband as a deliberate choice. It is an open decision. She does not have to assume that she is trapped in a marriage as a child. The "closed marriage" of previous generations would have made this assumption. She would have been advised to bear her suffering, assume her cross, do her part without complaining. But those assumptions of servitude are no longer acceptable in upper middle-class circles. Mrs. Polk wants to be herself. But until now she has not realized that being a self in marriage was her own deliberate choice. She can decide (1) to remain a child in marriage, (2) to move out of the marriage, or (3) to change her relationships within the marriage.

As she discussed these choices, Mrs. Polk decided that the first was clearly unacceptable. She was unwilling to continue a relationship in which fits of anger and days of sulking were interpreted by her husband as signs of infantile behavior. She would have to talk with him as an adult.

The second possibility was somewhat appealing. One of her physicians had advised her to focus attention upon her work and to think less of her marriage. He considered her to be a very talented person who could go far in the business world: "He told me my creativity was being frustrated in household duties and caring for my husband. He wasn't necessarily telling me to get a divorce, but I really thought about that possibility. Anyway, I'm not going to act on that right now, because I love my husband and I think we can really get something out of our marriage if we try."

Mrs. Polk decided to work on the third possibility, which was a deliberate choice to become an adult with her husband.

Deliberate choice is a characteristic of friendship. Perhaps, the freedom of choice led Mrs. Polk to act more like a friend with her husband. She was less of the moody, touchy wife who assumed that she was trapped in marriage. She was now beginning to share a little bit of herself as she would with a friend, to whom it would be natural to say, "I'm tired."

In the third interview Mrs. Polk did not look very fresh. She reported six days of heart pain. There was also a feeling of fishhooks in her throat. She had consulted a medical specialist, who conducted an examination that terrified her. She was not to drink anything for twelve hours before the examination. During the examination she lay head down on the X-ray table in the dark. She felt as if she was smothering and had to have something to drink.

Now she wondered if she were emotionally sick. Her husband had told her she probably was. Now she wanted a psychological answer. When the counselor did not give her a yes or no, she said: "Well, I think you know the answer and you're just not telling me." When the counselor asked how she felt about this frustration she replied: "I feel the same way I feel about marrying you. I don't like the idea. You are able to look through people as though they were transparent. You know the answer but are holding back on me." This led to a rather heated exchange:

DR. RICH: Ah so, you pushed me for an answer just like you push your husband.

MRS. POLK: Just what do you mean by pushing?

DR. RICH: You put me and the husband in a double bind, I bet. You say that you want to be independent and then you keep asking us for final answers to your questions.

MRS. POLK: The trouble with you men is that you're all evasive. You want to have the power but you won't take any of the responsibility.

DR. RICH: Yes, and if we do take the responsibility, you try to change the decision. I suspect that you may set up your husband by telling him that he's supposed to make decisions, then cutting him down when they don't suit you.

MRS. POLK: Ha! If I could get him to make a decision, how happy I would be. At least he's beginning to do a few things since I talked to him last week. Oh, I wouldn't place confidence in what he does but it's a try for now.

DR. RICH: So you really don't have much confidence in him?

MRS. POLK: Why should I? It's difficult to live with someone who has wanted to die since he was twelve years old. He had some kind of problem then that made him unconscious for several days. He says he felt as though he was out of his hospital room for several days, even though his body was still there. He said he had never had any particular incentive for anything after that. His soul left his body and has never been reconnected, I guess.

DR. RICH: Well, this is the first time I have ever heard such a graphic description of a headless or heartless husband.

MRS. POLK: Oh, I'm not saying that he has no heart. He's just thoughtless. When my father died it was quite a shock to me and I called him [the husband] in a panic. His answer over the phone was: "My God, what a time for me to have to leave the office!" That's all he said!

DR. RICH: Did you tell him how this hurt you?

MRS. POLK: No, no, I stopped that years ago. I used to get into a tirade, and he would listen until he got tired and then shut me off.

DR. RICH: I don't quite see why the two of you have stayed together as long as you have. You don't seem to value him very highly, and from your report he doesn't place much value on your feelings.

MRS. POLK: I don't know. Maybe some things can change. Anyway I want to keep my marriage.

The interview was ended. Mrs. Polk gave a little sigh and walked out of the office. She seemed a little glassy-eyed, as though something had just struck her that would require much thought before she could give any answer.

At least something had struck the counselor. He had concluded the interview with the second characteristic of friendship in equalitarian marriage. This is the valuing of another person as highly as ourselves. There is no thought of making up for a lack in another person or of finding protection in that person or of enjoying dominance. All of these thoughts were characteristic of Mrs. Polk. She wanted very much to make decisions and to do things that were not done by her husband. She wanted the protection of his decisions or the decisions of her counselor. At the same time she enjoyed the feeling that she was more adequate than her husband. Unless she can find some characteristic in him that she values as highly as her own, people will continue to ask her, "Why do you stay in this marriage?"

In the next interview, Mrs. Polk showed that she had been thinking about some things also. She announced: "I've been thinking about my attitudes toward men—and I guess I should tell you about them. I don't believe a woman can express her feelings around men. They don't like to see scenes and they quickly react against them. The men do this because they can't stand strong emotion. I have never known any man in my life who was able to take strong emotion from me and to quiet me down. In fact, they always went to pieces or backed away from me. So, that's just the way it is."

DR. RICH: Sounds like you're trapped in your own idea about men. Now you don't express your feelings around them, for their sakes.

MRS. POLK: Well, when things happen, you learn not to do the same thing again. It's like we said several sessions ago, it's bad to be frustrated and say nothing but it's worse to talk and have no one pay attention to you. It's not just my stupid husband. My boss is the same way. He doesn't want any women coming in to see him about business matters. He tells me to take care of all the women for him. It's the same way with the other men there at the office. They can't take care of women customers, or colleagues, or even of the secretaries. Of course, they don't say they're frightened by the women. No, no, they say women are excitable, flighty creatures with lots of emotion and that there is no place for emotion in the business.

DR. RICH: So why is it that they confide in you?

MRS. POLK: Because they say that I'm calm and collected, not like those other women.

DR. RICH: So, by acting differently from other women you get what you want out of the men?

MRS. POLK: Well, yes, I guess I just know how to use them.

DR. RICH: This is satisfying at work, but somehow does not give the same satisfactions at home?

MRS. POLK: That's right. I shouldn't have to be pulling my husband around this way or that. I need someone who can handle me when I get into a bad mood. But I am the one who is always handling him. It's just awful! I want him to take the lead and he never does.

DR. RICH: What's the possibility of some agreement between you on these things? I mean, maybe there are some areas in which he should take the lead and some areas where you should. Have you discussed any of that?

MRS. POLK: What do you mean discuss it? A man should know what he is supposed to do as a husband and father. Am I supposed to tell him about those things? How could I respect him then?

DR. RICH: Easy, easy, I'm just trying to raise some questions that might help. I just think that maybe you're expecting some things of him that he doesn't expect of himself. Or maybe he does and just can't do it. I mean, maybe there would be more respect between you if you figured out the areas in which each of you have something to contribute.

There were other topics in this interview, but this one is enough to illustrate the importance of a third characteristic of friendship in marriage. This is the fidelity of friends based on mutual admiration rather than on social convention. Dr. Rich does not believe that the marriage of Mr. and Mrs. Polk will work if it is based on the usual conventions of society. She expects him to be a dominant, successful male and he does not sound like that kind of person. She would certainly be frustrated if he were, for she has plenty of aggressive needs that must find expression. If she were trapped within a conventional marriage, there would be some explosions. As it is, she probably cuts him down to the size that she really wants. Then she complains that he is not living up to her high expectations of a dominant male.

The counselor will have to work some more on the social conventions. Mrs. Polk does not feel comfortable with equality. She still thinks that her marriage will look better if he appears to be in control. And, although this would be realistic and helpful in some marriages, she thinks that it should be true for all marriages and most especially for hers.

This is where some discrimination must be made in our model of marriage. In her particular case, dominance by the male is most inappropriate. Equal partnership is more realistic. But to accept this, Mrs. Polk must drop her childhood assumptions of the man in control. And to do this, she will have to give up some of her conclusions about many of the men with whom she has worked, and the one with whom she now lives. She thinks that they desire the illusion of control and that she must put up with this in order to survive.

The question of the expectation about men came up indirectly in a later interview. Mrs. Polk was criticizing the advice of one of her medical specialists who had said that she should separate from her husband. She needed a new world of her own.

DR. RICH: That's a rather direct statement to come from a physician. Are you sure it was that way?

MRS. POLK: Of course I'm sure. But at least I waited until I was with you to talk about it. I didn't go home and talk with my husband about it. Of course, that's the way doctors are. They always tell you what they think, whether they know the circumstances or not. Isn't that just like a man?

DR. RICH: Well, if you felt so strongly about it, what did you have to say to him about it?

MRS. POLK: I did not dignify his comment with an answer! I don't have any particular feelings about what he said. It was really not his business.

DR. RICH: I'm not so sure you have no feelings about this kind of remark from a man in authority.

MRS. POLK: Well, after all, there's no reason why you should be able to give me an answer either. You haven't met my husband and you don't know what the circumstances are that may be with us five years from now. It's unfair to ask you for a decision. His remarks certainly didn't make any sense to me and I doubt that yours would either. This is something I have to work out with my husband. I am certainly not going to get into that again with a doctor by telling him about it.

DR. RICH: So you will keep this to yourself?

MRS. POLK: Yes. I think he is an excellent physician and as far as helping me with my physical condition is concerned, I'll continue to go to him. As far as my husband is concerned, there's no need to talk to him about any question like what I'm to do with my energy or what I might do about our marriage. We're getting along better than we have in years. I don't intend to tell him that I am more intelligent than he is and that he can't understand everything that I do. There are some things to be conserved in our marriage that are worthwhile. It would be destructive for me to lay it all out the way that I do with you.

DR. RICH: Well, you do have some very positive feelings for your husband! I didn't think so in our last interview. (*Pause.*) I believe that you have the ability to distinguish those areas in which your doctor has authority and those in which he does not. (*Mrs. Polk nods in affirmation.*) It also appears that you think there are some values in your husband worth conserving in your marriage, even though there are some ways in which you think you know more than he does. (*Mrs. Polk nods again.*)

This affirmation of the husband was a surprise to Dr. Rich. It opened the possibility of some future discussion of another characteristic of friendship in marriage. That is, the sharing of time, talents, possessions. This would be the opposite of traditional expectations that the wife is owned by her husband.

The decisions for sharing between equals might be very informal and casual or they might be as thorough as those of Alix and Martin Schulman. In a section on

"The Marriage Experiments," April 28, 1972, *Life* magazine presented the principles and the job breakdown for the Schulman family.

I. PRINCIPLES

1. We reject the notion that the work which brings in more money is the more valuable. The ability to earn more money is already a privilege which must not be compounded by enabling the larger earner to buy out of his/her duties.

2. We believe that each member of the family has an equal right to his/her time, work, value choices. If he/she wants to use it making money, fine. If he/she wants to spend it with spouse, fine. If not, fine.

3. As parents we believe that we must share all responsibility for taking care of the children and home—not only the work, but the *responsibility*.

4. In principle, jobs should be shared equally, 50–50, but deals may be made by mutual agreement. Any deviation from 50–50 must be for the convenience of both parties. The schedule should be flexible, but for the time being, changes must be formally agreed upon. The terms of this agreement are *rights* and *duties*, not *privileges* and *favors!*

II. JOB BREAKDOWN

Children

Mornings: Waking children; getting out clothes, notes, homework, money, bus passes, books, brushing their hair; giving them breakfast (making coffee for us). Every other week each parent does all.

Baby sitters must be called by the parent the sitter is to replace. No sitter, parent stays.

Helping with homework etc. wife does between 3 and 6 p.m. After six husband does Tuesday, Thursday and Sunday. Other days wife does except Friday which is free for whoever has done extra work.

Weekends: wife is free all Sunday.

Housework
Laundry: Wife does home laundry, husband picks up cleaning. She strips beds, he remakes them.

Cooking: whoever invites guests does shopping, cooking and dishes.

Shopping: generally wife does daily food shopping, husband does special shopping.

Children's agreement
Polly sets the table and Teddy clears. Sometimes they swap their chores as do their parents. Ted also sorts and folds the laundry.

Children
Weekends: All usual child care, plus special activities (beach, park, zoo) split equally. Husband free all Saturday, wife free all Sunday.

The Schulmans give a thorough picture of how they will share in marriage without surrendering individuality. Each person contributes something, and no one is required to give everything.

A formal contract may seem too calculated in our modern world of informality and spontaneous emotion. I would agree that a written contract is not necessary to obtain the effect of sharing without surrender. But I would remember that some formal contracts have been used for thousands of years to preserve some freedom for women within marriage. From the most ancient records of the Old Testament until the present time, there have been agreements between families on the contribution of the father to the household of his daughter and the conditions under which she and that contribution would return to the father. It may have been camels in the day of Abraham and a decision about household labor in the days of the Schulmans. Whatever the time, the principle is the same: something must be reserved for each partner.

Talk about dowries and contracts will be objectionable to those who expect a marriage without reservations. But the reservation qualities, either physical or psychological, are symbols of our freedom to share, to give what we have to another person under conditions that respect their individuality and ours.

But this "holding out" may sound like a lack of faith. Do we really believe that this marriage is going to work? Yes, within limitations. In this chapter we have considered the limitations of individuality. In the next chapter we will see how hope will be realistic when it is restrained within institutional bounds. The reasonableness of our expectations will determine the wise distribution of our psychological resources and the gratitude with which another person receives our affection.

5

Interpret Your Dreams

Hope is an enduring belief that our fervent desires may be fulfilled despite inner conflicts and external adversity. It is wish fulfillment within the range of reality.

Unrealistic romances founder on the shallow assumption that all dreams will come true. Early expectations are unrealized. Because of this disillusionment, couples may grow cynical and their marriage may sour.

How can a modern couple expect to find intimate fulfillment over a lifetime with marriage as they have known it? The question is answered with a sense of hopelessness with the existing institution by writers such as the O'Neills, who do not see how "absolute fidelity" can be maintained as men and women grow and reach the free expectations of society. The dropout wife, Wanda Lee Adams, found no hope in the continuation of her marriage to a devoted husband and her association with her three children. Author Robert Rimmer encourages relationships outside marriage because modern society is experimental and open to the future. Mr. Rimmer believes that women are more open to "structured adultery" than are men because women are more "secure" about their sexuality. He has received letters from hundreds of women who would like to move into a triangular relationship but are frustrated by a jealous husband.

The alternative life-styles of the 1970's offer hope for women who are lonely and for men who are frustrated. Mr. Rimmer believes that group cohabitation will give the lonely college girl a chance to come out of her dormitory room and enjoy an occasional evening in bed with a male classmate. The young male will have his strong desires satisfied through two or three female admirers. Everybody will be more satisfied and the future family will be stronger.

I would agree with the revisionists of modern marriage that their alternative life-styles will offer more opportunities for lonely and frustrated people to look for temporary affection. It seems that this will be a new source of hope for those who despair in monogamy. But the transitory and ambiguous relationships of group cohabitation will make hope an illusion. Hope cannot live without faith, and the modern life-styles are not built upon faithful relationships. This lack of permanence came out of one question in *Psychology Today* with Mr. Rimmer: "How many couples do you know who have stayed together for several years?" Mr. Rimmer knew of four couples so far. It would seem that his best sellers *The Harrad Experiment* and *The Rebellion of Yale Marratt* have brought in many letters, but have not provided stability for a new form of family. Mr. Rimmer admitted that monogamy was superior to group marriage when there was a need for interpersonal adjustments. Neurotic problems are accentuated in group marriage. A monogamous marriage can be held together by the children.

When we begin to talk about children and other responsibilities, hope takes on a different meaning. Hope means one thing to a man who is looking for a mistress and something else to a man such as Mr. Park, who tries to give meaning and joy to his family while Mrs. Park recovers from a depression.

Hope is giving love time to take root. It is the cheerful delay of some gratification. A person does not insist on the immediate gratification of all his impulses. Even such basic desires as affirmation must not run wild in a continual demand for affection. I saw this in one thirty-five-year-old man who asked help in getting his wife back into the home. When I asked why she had moved out he answered: "I guess no woman could stand the pressure. I kept demanding that she affirm me all the time. I've never felt accepted. I thought this time, with a second marriage, it would be perfect. I kept demanding that it would be that way with my new wife. Finally, she told me that she couldn't give all the time. She said that my love smothered her."

The husband could never give love time to take root. He had no faith in himself. Faith is the foundation upon which hope rests, and hope also nourishes and sustains faith. If the husband can learn to stand the anxiety of waiting for affection, he probably will be rewarded. That for which he hoped will then sustain the faith that he is developing.

Delayed gratification is a new word for patience. It is the ability to watch and wait for the fruits of love.

We do not pull up the roots and examine them every day. This admonition is necessary any time when group sensitivity and marathon sessions encourage uncertain people to "examine their relationships" for days on end. Marriage is not a marathon therapy session. It is a small world for comfort and nurture along with growth and giving. We need some time to set our roots without disturbance. During that time there may be some mystery to our partner and some darkness in our own understanding. But we cannot reexamine everything all the time. In many cases we watch and wait. Weeks may go by before we see identified change in ourselves or in other persons.

I experienced this patience from other people when I was younger, without understanding it. I remember my return after college to the home of a family with whom I had lived when I was a sophomore. As I concluded my return visit, the lady of the house remarked that college had done me good. She was pleased to see my new sense of direction and security. She smiled and I could tell that she was pleased. Later I reflected on my false starts and impulsive assumptions when I lived with this family. They did not sit me down for long talks about my flippant ways, although it would have been good for someone to have done so at the time. Instead, they kept a steady relationship with me and were pleased to see their hope fulfilled at a later time. I doubt that they would have endured me without the thought of my eventual improvement.

Hope is based on faith that we can endure together until persons or situations change. It is a belief that we can still attain our goals even when life gets hard. We formalize and fortify hope against days of despair by institutionalizing relationships. There are public announcements of engagements, marriage licenses, birth certificates, university diplomas, business contracts. Each of these formal statements acknowledges the faithful relationship that underlies hope of fulfillment. We commit ourselves today for tomorrow.

The Limited Possibilities of Passion

I believe in hope within the institution of monogamous marriage. I place this virtue within a limited contract for two psychological reasons. First, we need some social reinforcement of our original declarations of commitment. There will be some difficult times in marriage and the internal bonds may be strained. External pressure can hold people together until they have untangled some of the personal difficulties that may arise in a young or even in a mature marriage. One of the staff members who read this manuscript made the comment that she certainly recognized the importance of a *social* contract after two years of marriage. In the first year she had thought that all was bliss. And now she thinks that some parts of marriage are a bore. But she is learning to make some adjustments to the responsibilities of marriage and to find satisfaction in the continuation of relationships that are now routine. She affirms that this is easier because she has made a commitment to this man before many witnesses and it is up to the two of them to work things out. She thought of other people her age who hopped from bed to bed when they were bored. She could not think of herself as being better than these former classmates. The difference was that she had a specific commitment and was not willing to give it up.

The young lady was also emphasizing the second psychological reason for hope to develop within an institution. She said that "you cannot have a satisfying relationship without commitment. There are some basic needs that are only satisfied in a family, like affection, nurture, recognition as a person. If you are not fully committed to another person, you cannot expect those intimate rewards over a long period of time. You have to be willing to give as much as you get."

The depth of commitment will determine the height of satisfaction in a relationship. A forty-year-old woman had this comment: "I have a full life with my husband. We have just been married for two years, but I can see all the difference in the world between my inner feelings now and five years ago. I felt like there was a hole inside of me then. I was divorced and went to parties as a way of filling up the time. People seemed to be very happy at the parties. I saw the same people at one party after another. They were so happy at the party, but when I met them individually on other occasions, they were just as empty inside as I was. They were good people but they did not have a partner to love and live for. There was no one person who really cared what happened to them. We were like people who always ate sweets when what we really needed were steaks."

Søren Kierkegaard said that hope is a passion for what is possible. I would add that hope in marriage is strongest when a limit is set on possibility. One of these limitations has already been discussed. Men and women expect to meet as many of their sexual needs as they can within marriage. They are not to hope for gratification outside that institution. Similarly, children are to expect acceptance and affection in a family. They cannot hope for the same love and trust in other relationships, although this sometimes may be provided. Their hope is to move from the warmth and security of mother and father to a kindred relationship with a husband and, in time, their own children. Marriage and the family are institutions that limit love. We would be foolish to expect the same understanding and comfort from an employer, pastor, or professor as we would look for in husband, wife, mother, or father.

We keep hope realistic by restraining it within institutional bounds. The reasonableness of our expectations within marriage is a key to many problems in counseling. We unlock psychological doors by asking: "What are your goals for this marriage?" "What were you taught to expect in a husband [wife]?" When I asked this question of a wife she replied that her husband should have the business sense of her father. Her husband should be able to provide an adequate income for family needs. He should be generous and yet tell her when she had reached the limit of spending for that month. She could charge things, but he should check on her charges. Since her husband did not live up to her expectations, she felt justified in losing respect for him.

Another counselee had even grander expectations of her husband. She said: "I would think that a man should be able to handle his business in a reasonable period of time during any one day and still be a leader in civic affairs and pay attention to his family. My father was always able to do this. But Frank—he spends twice as much time as any other manager at his desk. He's just slow."

These wives are hoping for perfect "fathers" in a

marriage. They are obviously disappointed. They have made premature and self-willed decisions about marriage. This is one of the two forms of sin against hope that are mentioned by Josef Pieper. It is the error of presumption. We decide what we are going to expect before we know what can be realistically offered. Theologically we see this presumption in people who hope that God will do anything they desire. Psychologically, we find husband and wife expecting the mate to conform to the pattern of a father or a mother, or a successful brother or an affectionate sister. It is a false hope because we are not loving the person for what he really is. We love that which we have left behind and we require our present partner to be an adequate substitute.

This parental fixation mars any marriage. Jesus detected this error when he said that a man was to leave his mother and father and cleave to his wife and the two of them were to be one flesh.

Since husband and wife are often unaware of all of their expectations in marriage, what is to happen when we find that either one of us does not measure up? In *The Theology of Hope,* Jürgen Moltmann quotes a second form of sin that has been enunciated by Josef Pieper. This is despair, a premature and arbitrary decision that we are not going to receive what we hope for. Theologically this is a lack of faith in God. Psychologically it is a lack of faith in ourselves or in those who love us.

One sign of despair is the assumption that all things are wrong because one thing did not work out right. Dr. Harris, in his book *I'm OK—You're OK,* stated that a childish person will expect perfection. When there is any disappointment in himself or in those to whom he is committed, he descends into despair and says, "Nothing ever works out right."

An adult would accept some imperfection. We cannot control all the circumstances that mar our lives, but we do have some responsibility for our reaction to unanticipated events. When we have been trained to accept some emergencies, we can recoup our losses more gracefully and maintain optimism. Ezra Stotland in *The Psychology of Hope* reports a study of submarine sailors who were prepared for various emergencies. They were not caught off guard by the inevitable mishaps of a voyage and so experienced little anxiety. Conversely, untrained personnel were distraught in the same situations and felt completely helpless.

In marriage, we should expect some disagreements and disappointments. When we see that these problems are accepted by mature people whom we admire, we will take hope that our marriage may survive despite occasional anger and misinterpretation. The marital problem of many adults is an inability to anticipate or accept the little traumas of life. When the toddler steps on a Christmas ornament, the mother's happiness has gone to pieces. If the husband does not come home in time for tennis, his wife can think of nothing else to do but be blue.

There are two limitations of hope in marriage. First, the institution limits a person's expectations. Second, I have emphasized the acceptance of limitations in ourselves and in those whom we love. If we can expect a little less than the best, we can hope more realistically for what is actually available. The model statement would be that of God to Noah as recorded in *Green*

Pastures. When Noah realized that he was speaking to the Almighty he fell on his knees and said, "Lord, I ain't much, but I'se all that I got."

An acceptance of limitations in ourselves and in others is the beginning of hope as is expressed both in counseling practice and in Biblical theology. In the Bible, hope is always related to the human condition of sin. Athough we deserve condemnation, we have confidence in God because of his forgiveness. The Biblical writers always reckon with the worst, a moral relationship to be redeemed. They continue with courage because of their faith in God. He will support us despite our own sin and our misfortunes in the world.

Hope: Past, Present, and Future

Biblical hope is anchored in history. The Hebrews always reassured themselves by references to their deliverance by God from Egypt. The New Testament writers found strength despite adversity in the news of Christ's resurrection (I Cor. 15:19–20; Eph. 1:18–20; I Peter 1:3–13). At first, the most vivid Christian hope was in the immediate return of the Lord. We find this expectation in such early writings of Paul as I Thessalonians. In the later writings of Paul, another source of hope appears, the anchoring of our lives in a plan that God has developed for us from the beginning of time. This is the first message of his Letter to the Ephesians. It is also the proclamation of Rom. 5:1–5.

I find a parallel to the theological plan of Paul in the psychological development of a healthy marriage. In our first months or years of marital bliss we expect the immediate fulfillment of all the dreams and promises of courtship. There is much fulfillment, but there is also some disappointment. Gradually we realize that we cannot be everything that we wished to be to each other. We are strongly conditioned by the images of our own parents. This may be a growing source of either pleasure or disappointment. In any case, we are beginning to look back farther into the roots of character. We find that many of our present attitudes and actions are dependent upon events before our own time. This is most markedly demonstrated in the case of severe physical or emotional handicaps. In *The Etiology of Schizophrenia,* Dr. Mary Bowen found that an inadequate mother would develop a strong attachment to one child. This would substitute for her disappointment in her relationship with husband or parents. It was this child who most commonly became schizophrenic.

Numerous studies of birth defects have pointed up the same basic finding. People inherit much more than they expect from their parents. Some limitations are passed on from parents to children and to the children's children.

As we move farther into marriage, we become more aware of adequate or inadequate foundations in our home. Will this lead to hope or despair? If a person entertains the thought of completely changing himself or his mate, there will be severe despair. His great expectations cannot be realized. But if our thought moves like that of Paul, we will recognize the limitations of life for just what they are, conditioning influences. If we know our resources and our obstacles from the past, we are in a better condition to move realistically toward the future. We can plan on the basis of that which is known but shape our expectations by that which is given.

This is a tricky point in marriage counseling. A person who does not want to change will seize on it as a last defense. One consultee, Mrs. Lake, declares that she now knows that she will never be able to demonstrate much affection. Her parents never did this, therefore her husband should not expect it of her. If he really loves her, he will accept her just as she is.

I asked her if she were willing for her husband to leave, since he could not stand the continued barriers between them, which included separate bedrooms. She said that if he attacked her any more about personal deficiencies, she would be willing to separate. However, she quickly added that there was no sense in him getting uptight about things that would not change. He should accept her as a person who has nothing to say to him and does not wish to express affection to anyone but the children.

My next step will be to help Mrs. Lake see why she is so frightened. It is true that she has a very restricted background, but this does not mean that she cannot make some adjustment to the affirming needs of husband and wife at the present time. I suspect that some incident within the last year or two has hurt Mrs. Lake and discouraged her husband. When I know this rankling secret, or they have discussed it privately, I believe she will not be so fatalistic.

The Christian church has an anecdote for fatalism in the doctrine of the Holy Spirit. Here is a source of continual change and personal growth. As Paul puts it in Rom. 8:26: "Likewise the Spirit helps us in our weakness; for we do not know how to pray as we ought, but the Spirit himself intercedes for us with sighs too deep for words."

We are not to give way to weakness and become resigned in despair. Instead, we are to "wait with patience" for the fulfillment of our hopes through the spirit of God.

We attack fatalism in marriage by a concentration upon the present. When Mrs. Lake uses the past to justify her frozen position in the present, I will ask how this makes her appear to herself and to others in the here and now. What kind of person has she become? Is she aware of how rigid, controlled and lifeless she appears? Is this what she hopes for herself?

We have already begun to discuss something like this. In a joint interview, Mr. Lake told how he had recently become interested in music and painting. These had never been subjects of interest in his family. Mrs. Lake sat and stared at him. I asked what she thought of her husband's interest. She said: "Well I guess that's all right. Some of my friends think he's quite interesting. He made some remark about the soloist in a recent concert that really cracked up a friend of mine. She has told everybody what he said. But so what, what's that suppose to mean to me?"

I said that it might mean a change in her perception of Frank. Perhaps he was a more interesting husband than she had seen in the past. "So," she said, "should I tell him that? What good would it do?" I looked at Mr. Lake. He said: "No good. I'd just be angry that she has thought for so long that I wasn't interesting."

I then made a speech about the importance of starting with small favors to each other. Both parties were expecting too much. They would need to learn a system of small rewards on a daily basis. Mrs. Lake can affirm her husband in some specific way, such as a comment on his new interest in music and art. He can accept this as one sign that she grants him some competence.

This may not work. They are so negative toward each other that she will probably sneer when she compliments him and he will be mad that she does not completely accept him. They want so much that they cannot get a little.

I tried to keep these people in conversation by a third part of hope, which is the wider future dimension. Very little will be accomplished now, but we can lay the basis in the present for more practice in the future. Do not promise immediate release of tension. Note the contradictions and oppositions that are now present, and suggest some of the ways people have used to reduce these problems over a period of time. Promise to stay with the people as an instructor and helper during this period, if they are willing. Do not set the goals for their future, but help them overcome despair about the attainment of those goals.

In the midst of these conflicts, a counselor offers creativity. He shares his images of their relationships and trys to evoke their own. I said to Mr. and Mrs. Lake: "I have the fantasy of two people who have a controlled space around them. There is a gulf between your controlled space. It is as though you were placed in a house side by side, but were seldom in contact with each other." The couple thought that my image was accurate and added their own feeling about the current isolation.

MR. LAKE: But we've known this about each other for some time. We tell these things to each other, but nothing changes.

COUNSELOR: You're well defended against each other. Each of you says something that is correct, but in a way that the other cannot accept. For example, you tell your wife that she should be strong and never give in to her feelings. Is that what you do?

MR. LAKE: Yes, I tell her, but it doesn't seem to do any good.

COUNSELOR: Why doesn't the speech do any good, Mrs. Lake?

MRS. LAKE: I am not in any state to hear what he says when he says it. I know he's right, but I just don't have control of myself right then.

COUNSELOR: If he does not say these things at the right time, then I would guess that he does not really understand what is going on inside you.

MRS. LAKE: Well, no, he doesn't. He doesn't feel things like I do. Nothing ever seems to bother him. There are times when everything bothers me.

COUNSELOR: And at those times, you are also bothered by his inability to understand what is happening in you.

MRS. LAKE: I guess so. I know I feel worse and sometimes I explode at him. (*Pause.*) Then of course I feel even worse the next day.

COUNSELOR: Mr. Lake, how much do you know about despair and guilt in yourself?

MR. LAKE: I know what it's like. My father was a nothing and I was a nothing. I have tried to build myself up. I know what she's talking about but I make speeches to myself about keeping control and that helps. If I have feelings that I can't manage, then I try to forget about them. I just give up that part of myself.

COUNSELOR: Ugh. You're cutting off pieces of yourself because they don't seem to fit.

MR. LAKE: (*Smiles faintly.*) Yes, I guess I thought I must do that to be successful. Do you think I am pushing aside some parts of myself that would help keep us together?

COUNSELOR: That's a good thought. Look, if you are going to understand her despair, you'll have to be in contact with your own. If you throw away anything that depresses, you'll never understand what your wife and many other people are going through.

MR. LAKE: You mean I'm not really in contact with her feelings because I'm not in contact with myself?

COUNSELOR: Right, right, it sounds to me as though you have already been through some sessions like this before.

MR. LAKE: Oh yes, we were trained as volunteer counselors for the crisis center in Sacramento. We studied transactional analysis. I learned that one of the major problems with my wife is that she is not an O.K. person. That's the way she always sees herself. I try to tell her that she is O.K.

COUNSELOR: Maybe you'd better try telling that to yourself first.

MRS. LAKE: Oh, he is a wonderful counselor. People call him in a crisis and he can really help them over the telephone. But when he's at home . . . (*She shrugs her shoulders and smiles.*)

COUNSELOR: Each of you seems to know the other well, but you haven't yet learned how to make that knowledge work for your mutual benefit. I guess my role is to help find ways for you to fit together.

There are two ways in which we can help to provide hope for people. One is through guidance and instruction. They can believe with us that there are some ways through the labyrinth of their current frustrations. We can seek actively to explain *some* of the problems. We cannot explain everything, but always encourage their attempts to speak first. When a couple go round and round in circles, try to show them some reasonable alternatives.

Secondly, a counselor can make his explanations without shaming the couple. Mr. and Mrs. Lake are now very ashamed of themselves. She feels that no good wife should be in so much despair. He wonders why his many attempts to train his wife in a rigid way of thinking have not been successful.

Try to be more factual and still appreciate some of their feelings. What they say does not sound shameful, just sad. They are not stupid or sinful, we can make them aware of our positive regard for them.

Positive regard is not the same as total approval. I think that Mr. Lake is too rigid and I let him know this in several ways. Occasionally I preach to him so that he will correct his applications of religion to life. If Mrs. Lake says that she feels guilty about screaming at the children, I will nod and say that a sensitive mother would feel guilty about such a lack of control. But she can come to understand the pressures leading to her loss of control and not feel that she is a totally unacceptable person because of this reaction.

There is a good deal of research to support the infusion of hope through the competence of others, such as a counselor. Ezra Stotland reported negative and positive influence of this. The negative side was an epidemic of suicides among mental hospital patients who had received no helpful communications from the people who attended them. On the positive side, people in other institutions said that they were helped because the staff comprehended the seriousness of their problems and provided a realistic evaluation of what must be done to overcome present difficulties.[14]

As we seek to restore hope to people in distress, we must look for the unrealistic expectations that have actually reduced hope. Myers and Roberts found that families with a schizophrenic child were those who placed the heaviest demands on children, setting very high and often unattainable goals for them regardless of their ability.[15]

If I am successful in my counseling with Mr. and Mrs. Lake, I imagine that they will soon begin to talk about the expectations that their parents had for them, or the goals that they set early in life on the basis of what they saw in their own home. When we have evaluated as adults the goals they set as children, we will be closer to a realistic basis for hope.

Hope will be stable and growing if we can connect a realistic evaluation of our expectations with some unified scheme of action. That is, we must identify attainable goals for people and help them marshal resources for progressive attainment of their dreams. Dreams can come true. We encourage people to tell us the heights or depths to which they would attain and then ask how their abilities match up with these objectives. In the process of these conversations, we enable people to explain themselves. They really develop a philosophy of life. We want the highest order of explanation to go with the deepest awareness of self.

The statement may sound contradictory. On the one hand we are asking people to be realistic in their self-estimate, to look at themselves without shame. Does this not lower their ideals and standards? Not necessarily. It only makes their goals reasonable. We move from a stage of sensuality, in which people are explaining their basic drives and wants, to a second stage of sociability, in which people describe the pleasures and social rewards that they seek in life. Finally, we move to a religious stage in which people explain their goals in terms of commitment to others for the sake of a power beyond themselves. This is where religious faith and hope are combined. We ask people to hope in something beyond themselves, beyond their family, beyond their society. We seek to place their ultimate trust in a completely reliable Being. This is the only hope that will really endure in the day of tribulation. His love is the only steadfast comfort under some conditions.

Dreaming Without Disgust

The conditions of modern marriage will seldom fulfill all our dreams. When the romantic ideas of courtship are compromised by the recognizable imperfections of a mate, either or both persons may become disgusted. There may be a sense of shame in looking for so much and attaining so little.

High emotional expectations can be handled in an open relationship. People can be encouraged to tell each other: "I had thought that we would always do things this way, but I am disappointed to find that it is not working out"; or, "I think that you want me to be cheerful all the time, but this is really not possible." These frank statements are the basis for negotiation toward an endurable and enduring relationship. They are affirmations of who we are, even though we do not embody all the fantasies of our partner, or of ourselves.

Our dreams must be interpreted. They are vague symbols of our desire for a better life. But what do they mean in the context of this marriage relationship? Why do we persist in some fantasies and forget others? How many of our aspirations are actualized and how many of them are beyond possibility?

The intrepretation of dreams is most possible in a relationship of friendship. It is customary for most of us, from childhood, to share with close friends the fears of the future. We appreciate a friend who makes sense out of what we hope for. He or she will tell us that this is the kind of person we can become, or that we are just trying to model someone who has different talents. There is no thought that we are destroying a relationship by being honest about ourselves.

In contrast romantic expectations in marriage should not be interpreted in an aura of romance. This only increases the possibility of unreality in the dominant-dependent assumptions of traditional marriages. In a need-fulfillment marriage a person is made to feel guilty if he does not embody the dreams of his partner. Isn't this what marriage is supposed to be all about? The adequate person is supposed to meet all the needs of the inadequate one, and the less adequate one is to dream great dreams of satisfying the one who is worshiped.

It is natural for young lovers to think much of mutual gratification. But, I would hope that the desires of courtship would soon be combined with the realistic appraisal of people who are friendly enough to tell each other exactly what they can realize in this marriage. We like being loved when we are truthful about our dreams and see some of them grow into realistic satisfaction.

6

Enjoy Sex for Tomorrow

The dreams of romance can now be lived in the full light of day. The longings that were formerly whispered between lovers are now mottoes for movies. In 1948 *The New York Times* refused to carry a medical textbook publisher's advertisement for the first Kinsey report. But by 1970 *The New York Times* and other newspapers were carrying ads and reviews of books that were formerly in the locked library cases of the Kinsey Institute for Sex Research or the Z section of the Library of Congress.

The public discussion of intimacy in romance and marriage has included the search for both sexual and interpersonal competence. Intimacy and equality have grown together.

Progress toward public awareness of intimate feelings and actions has paralleled the push for equality of the sexes. The rights of women and the acknowledgment of inner cravings have been part of the twentieth century's surge toward new freedom.

The road toward inner freedom was blazed for secular society in the writings and teachings of Sigmund Freud. The signposts for psychoanalysis were forbidden words in polite Viennese society: oral, anal, phallic.

Inner freedom through sexual awareness sounded like an invitation to licentiousness in the early twentieth century. Knowledge of any forbidden pleasure was the original sin in the eyes of our ancestors. Innocence was equated with naïveté.

Freud and his associates were not libertines, but their doctrines of man were not the same as their Viennese neighbors'. The Freudians sought for inner control through self-knowledge. A person who knew the reasons for his actions would have more power to act in accordance with the goals of his life.

The early Freudians were unwilling to set goals for a patient's future. They would only investigate the past blocks to his present fulfillment of life. Later Freudians, like Karen Horney, connected goals in living to health and neurosis. To Dr. Horney, the neurotic personality of our time was a person who was absorbed in self-glory. A healthy person had goals in life that did as much for society as they did for himself.

The preoccupation of Sigmund Freud had been with the inner processes of the mind. Analysts concentrated upon the feelings of one person. It was unorthodox to talk with both husband and wife.

After World War II, intimacy entered a new phase. That which was formerly expressed only to the analyst was now to be communicated between husband and wife, parent and child, lovers and relations. "Interpersonal relationships" became a subject of concern in upper middle-class marriages and were soon the topics of chapters in high school texts on hygiene and health. "Family counseling" and "family therapy" became a school of thought in the 1960's with theories, practices, textbooks, and teachers. Intimacy was part of popular writing about marriage as in *The Intimate Enemy,* by George Bach, or *The Intimate Marriage,* by Howard and Charlotte Clinebell.

Intimacy and equality were assumed in these and related writings. Husband and wife were presumed to share equally in all the rights of marriage. They were trained to develop mutual adequacy and fulfillment.

Mutual adequacy and satisfaction were basic to the O'Neills' writing of *Open Marriage.* Their writing opened a door to a new stage in intimacy and equality, which was the recommendation that both partners will have growing relationships outside marriage as well as within marriage. These outside relationships may include sex. So far as the O'Neills are concerned, this decision is completely up to the partners involved.[16]

Friendly Intimacy

Should intimacy go as far as the O'Neills intimate? Yes and no.

The yes is for more intimate friendships. This is the relationship which needs to be strengthened. There was a time when many companionship needs were met between friends. Most of the biographies and autobiographies of the past one hundred years have stressed the influence of father, mother, and friends. These were the persons with whom a person shared his private thoughts.

Wife and children have been so neglected in biographies that the psychological biographer, Erik Erikson, once complained that men who made history never seemed to have families. At least this was the way their biographies read.

We face a curious reversal of intimate relationships in modern society. The private affairs of marriage are now subjects for public conversation. The public identification with friends has either disappeared or become private.

An open display of loyalty would be difficult among the upper middle classes today, even if it were desirable. For whom would a person proclaim his friendship? The intimate associations of roommates in an isolated college town have been replaced by the confusion of 10,000 students hurrying to evening classes in a community college that has no dormitories. Childhood and high school chums have been replaced by instant association with people who work for some company and must attend this party. As soon as we settle down with some good companions, there is another transfer. One of the reasons for this transfer is a move to break up the hoarding of good talent through the formation of mutual understanding among executives. A mobile society has replaced the intimate ties of historic friendship with immediate adaptation to associates for the moment.

New Forms of Friendship

How can intimate ties be maintained in the marriage and in the community under these shifting circumstances? The answer of some people is to refuse a transfer or to follow a line of work that emphasizes long-term relationships. For example, one airline company believes that the executives of a travel and vacation division should put down roots in one large city. As they meet community leaders, they develop friendships or contacts that bring in specific kinds of business during any one year. A company gains from the exact knowledge of the executive and his long-term association in one place. In contrast, another company rotates travel executives around the world. It believes that intimate knowledge of many places is the best qualification for a promotional executive.

Another way to expand intimacy is through growth groups. These may range from a weekend marathon to a year or more of group discussion. Such groups meet the need for intimate expression of feeling, which once would have been met through conversation with friends, and train lonely and inhibited people in the art of friendship. We learn, in these groups, how we feel, both for ourselves and for others.

If the group is developed for sick persons along psychotherapeutic lines, there will be little contact outside the weekly session. But if the group is organized for more or less healthy persons, it may facilitate enduring relationships. For example, a number of churches have followed the lead of the First Community Church in Columbus, Ohio, and developed interest groups for widows, young couples, parents with an "empty nest." These people take responsibility for each other as they become better acquainted. One class was organized for parents who were expecting their first child. When one of the couples lost their baby, the other couples were the major support of husband and wife during this trying time. Since they were alone in a large city, there was no one else to be their friends.

Friendship and intimacy have also been combined in communes. The most enduring of these have had some religious moorings. This provides some common goal and also limits exploitation of other people.

In the less-structured communes, exploitation of women is notorious. Women bitterly complain that they are treated as second-class citizens who are tolerated because of their sexual attractiveness or capacity for household labor. In these communes, equality has not kept pace with intimacy.

Another solution to intimacy and equality is serial monogamy. That is, people stay together as long as they are good companions and then divorce each other when more suitable companions are found.

Some couples elect to keep their marriage legal but add a few lovers. This is the group marriage that Robert Rimmer called the "open end" monogamous marriage at the graduate and faculty levels at college and universities.[17] Mr. Rimmer believes that some structure is necessary for social interaction. Therefore, a marriage should remain, with church sanction, but should envision a two- or three-couple relationship when it is desired.

Limiting the Relationships

Mr. Rimmer admits that monogamy can survive deteriorating interpersonal adjustments because children can give the relationship a sense of purpose. Children are one limitation to a completely open marriage. They are one of the reasons that we must say no to any proposal that would completely blend friendship and marriage.

The virtue of fidelity is required in parents in order that virtue may grow in the child. Erik Erikson describes the first of childhood virtues as hope, the encounter of an infant with trustworthy persons who respond to him with intake and contact.[18]

Hope establishes a basic quality of experience. The child believes that objects in the world can be endowed with trust. It is nourished by the adult faith that pervades patterns of care.

Childhood trust is shattered by parental adultery. As the research of Murray Bowen and others has shown, the health of a parent-child relationship depends upon the adequacy of bonding between husband and wife.[19] When there is an alteration in the trust of husband and wife, there is a shaking of the foundations of a child's world.

Is this "old-fashioned" affirmation appropriate in modern marriage? An alert reader may object to my limitation of intimate relationship. I have just argued for a marriage between equals that includes strong affection for friends. How can I now say that an open relationship with friends of the opposite sex will damage parent and child?

My answer is that the psychological quality of parent-child relationship demands exclusiveness. The child must believe that his continual need for intake and contact is based upon biological, emotional, spiritual contact of mother and father. They give freely to him because they have shared freely with each other. He is a part of them and they are a part of him. No one else can make that kind of claim upon the three of them. The only permissible extension of that bond is to another brother or sister. The first child can understand that deprivation only by seeing it as an extension of his own rights and privileges. He is to love his siblings as his parents love him.

The demand for intake and contact are so overwhelming in the early years of life that no other relationship can be compared to it. A mother feeds her baby, physically and emotionally, as no one else is fed. A father gives time and energy to a child of his own that would not be required of him by any other person. The exclusiveness of the bond is not only necessary for the health of the infant, it is also a protection for the psychological resources of parents. Parents give of themselves to children in commitment of resources far beyond that which we would expect in friendship. This was understood by previous generations by the very words of praise for friendship. The highest complaint to a friend was to say that his love approximated that of a brother or sister. The only blending of friendship-brotherhood-parenthood came in Hebrew law that required a brother to marry the widow of a deceased brother who had left no children. This was a guarantee of immortality. The Hebrew father lived on through his children.

But it would seem that the example of Hebrew law would raise a second objection to the exclusiveness of the parental sexual relationship. The patriarchs had several wives. Other societies, in that day and this, extend sexual relationships so that a man may be the father of children by several wives or a wife may have children by several fathers.

In previous generations the argument against polygamy was based on the damaging rivalries and jealousies of children. This was mirrored in the conflicts of several wives for the attention of one husband or vice versa.

This is a valid objection to polygamy, especially in a mobile modern society. When most of our relationships are based upon instant contacts and frequent changes, there need to be some basic bonds about which there is no dispute. The exclusive claim of a child upon two parents is the basis of trust in a shifting society. At a time when he was helpless, two people were totally committed to him. He does not have to require that kind of commitment of others as he grows older. He can accept the relative quality of other relationships because one basic need has already been met in his life.

A sophisticated person may object to the turning of the argument toward polygamy. Those who favor alternative styles of marriage are not thinking of multiple parenthood. The argument is for parenthood as culturally defined in Western society, with some additional strengths. One of these strengths would be affection with other partners, including sexual intercourse by consent of all concerned. This would be looked upon as a source of refreshment and strength for one or both partners. They would be more adequate parents because deficits in their relationship had been met from other sources. Birth-control devices would prevent this relationship from going beyond affection for the moment.

Additional support for this open kind of marriage can be found in anthropological studies. Professors Clellan Ford and Frank Beach stated in *Patterns of Sexual Behavior* that less than 16 percent of 185 societies had formal restrictions to a single male. Less than a third of these societies would wholly disapprove of both premarital and extramarital relationships.[20]

The quotation of these statistics may offer the same form of relief that came to many males in their reading of the first Kinsey report. An anxious person looked up the statistics for a particular type of behavior and was relieved to find that thousands of persons participated in an act that had given him some cause to worry.

I could not argue that adultery is "abnormal," when statistical studies in American and other cultures reveal the widespread nature of multiple sexual relationships. But I am saying that adultery in modern Western society damages the character of a child. The breaking of an exclusive bond between husband and wife is felt as a lack of trust by the child.

But it could be objected that this assertion is limited to the current form of monogamous marriage. Alternative life-styles include communes in which much effort is given to the care of everyone's children. But the reports from communes are mixed. Few of them are in existence for the span of childhood. The most stable are religious societies in which sexual restraints are as strong as I advocate, or more abstinent.[21]

The Symbol of Self-commitment

The strengthening of trust in a child is one reason for the limitation of sex to marriage. But an exclusive emphasis upon children would miss the modern possibility of sex for its own sake. Birth-control measures improve the possibilities of physical intimacy between equals without fear of parenthood. When there is no thought of children, why should friendly people limit their relationships?

The only lasting limitation to sexual relationships is theological. It is the belief that the act of coitus engages and expresses the whole personality. Sexual activity is a unique mode of self-disclosure and self-commitment.[22]

The formulation of this doctrine by Paul was as unique in the Greek world as it is appropriate today. The social attitudes, then and now, were favorable to venereal indulgence. Neither Greeks of the first century nor sophisticated secularists in the twentieth century would worry about extramarital relationships if these were conducted with kindness and reasonable decorum.

It will be exceedingly difficult to dislodge the sexual union of consenting adults on psychological or sociological grounds. These disciplines now contain active components of sex for the sake of relationships. The ultimate attainment of this viewpoint is a union of sexuality and healing. British sexologist Martin Cole uses his wife and other volunteers to teach men and women how to copulate successfully. Patients in the Institute of Sex Education and Research are assigned to one of the volunteer therapists. Sessions are confined to conversations until some relationship is established and the couple can then move on toward touching and embracing. After several more meetings for limited genital contact there is a culmination in intercourse.[23]

The Cole method may provide a sociological equivalent of the ancient temples of Baal and Aphrodite. In these temples sacred prostitutes combined spiritual feeling with physical pleasure. To the ancients, intercourse in a temple had mystical meaning.

The behavioral sciences have now provided a successor to the mystery cults, and within the same type of society. The psychological methods of Martin Cole or Fritz Perls and the theories of Albert Ellis are consistent with the modern emphasis upon sex as an interpersonal relationship. Sexual morality is no longer defined as abstinence from nonmarital intercourse. It is now judged on the basis of responsibility and regard for the rights of others. Both the ancient Greek and the modern psychological views of some authors would destroy institutional limitations upon sexuality and free persons to make individual judgment about the quality of each relationship.

The relationship theory has led liberal religious leaders to write, as did John A. T. Robinson, that "nothing of itself can always be labeled wrong." A popular young theologian, Harvey Cox, has refused to deliver a prepared answer on the question of premarital intercourse, because sexual relations may strengthen the chances of sexual success and fidelity in marriage. Therefore, the real question is "whether avoidance of intercourse beforehand is always the best preparation [for marriage]." [24]

Curiously enough, the answer of Paul to the Greeks was also based upon a theory of relationships that combine intimacy and equality. Male and female, husband and wife are "joint heirs of the grace of life." In the Christian faith, the distinction of sex and its consequences become relatively unimportant.[25]

It is the acts and the attitudes between men and women that are crucial in Christian morality. The expression of physical intimacy is an inextractable combination of act and attitude. This is the key concept of Paul's writing to the Corinthian church. Physical intercourse combines people in a personal relationship for which they must take spiritual responsibility.

The symbolic force of an act and the importance of related attitudes are clearly stated by such diverse authors as Sigmund Freud and Carl Rogers. The apostle Paul goes beyond psychology to proclaim that the most intimate relationships of life have divine meaning. Intercourse symbolizes a mystical union. It is a reminder of God's creation of man and man's ability to re-create himself in sex and parenthood. The act is also a symbol that men and women are made for each other. Each is dependent upon the other for re-creation.

The New Testament writers proclaim that this creative act was originally designed for one man and one woman. These two become one flesh in the sense of mutual sharing and concern. The definitive symbol of this union is sexual intercourse, which is also the sign and potential of their creativity.

Christianity limits sex to monogamous relationships because of a belief in the particular symbolism of intercourse. Psychological and theological relationships are combined.

Public and Particular

Can the particularity of sexual activity be maintained in the public atmosphere of twentieth-century America? Can we talk as openly about this intimate part of marriage as we formerly spoke of all aspects of friendship?

The moralists of the nineteenth century maintained that the exclusiveness of sex and marriage could be maintained only by secretness on the subject. Some of the undesirable results of that solution were hypocrisy, the continuation of a double standard and a splitting of sexual activity from interpersonal relations.

Public discussion of erotic behavior has helped to correct each of these problems. But we are now in danger of talking so much about sex that we are entering a new phase of the same old thoughts.

Sophisticated society has a new hypocrisy, that of the sexual athletes. Zest for and techniques in lovemaking are now considered to be marks of an adequate personality. Social pressure is strong in a liberated group against those who are inhibited or inadequate. Pity and scorn are heaped upon the impotent and the frigid.

The dynamics of hypocrisy remain the same from generation to generation. Freud and others demonstrated the relationship between hysteria, sex, and personal inadequacy. In this generation, Rollo May proclaims the same theme in *Love and Will.* Now the inadequacies are expressed in feverish sexual activity and bold denunciations of those who do not participate. A renunciation of the double standard has led women to copy the sexual mores of men. In a 1967 survey of college students on personal characteristics in mate selection, both male and female students rated chastity as the fifteenth most desirable characteristic. In a 1939 survey it was tenth. The total number of traits were eighteen. In both 1939 and 1967 the most highly desired characteristics were dependable character and emotional stability.[26]

A drop in the double standard has not led to an alarming increase of premarital and extramarital sex. At least this is the dominant opinion of researchers at the present time. But there is much debate around the conclusion of Ira Reiss:

> There is a widespread belief that much has changed in terms of premarital sex behavior in the last twenty to twenty-five years. However, the evidence from all the available major studies is in strong agreement that although attitudes have changed considerably during this period, that many areas of sexual behavior, such as premarital coital rates, have not.[27]

Instead of proclaiming: "I can do anything that a man is expected to do," both women and men should ask: "What is expected of responsible people?" The former comment is a holdover from traditional assumptions about love. The man was expected to be free and dominant, while the woman was to be restricted and submissive. By contrast, a union based on the assumption of friendship would seek the same high standards for equals.

The greatest benefit of open discussions about sex has been the emphasis upon interpersonal relationships. Responsible attitudes and sexual activity have been brought together. The danger is that attitude will be overemphasized and action will be obscured. There are theological and psychological dangers to this one-sided emphasis. The theological problem is a break in the solidarity of spirit-flesh. True union with another person is total. We must take as much responsibility for what we do as for what we feel.

The modern preoccupation is with feeling more than willing. Therefore, actions are excused if they feel good. We push aside questions of the will, such as: "What do I think about myself in this activity?" or "Is this action consistent with the goals and purposes of my life?"

The balance of pleasurable feeling with lifetime purpose was bluntly stated by a thirty-five-year-old woman in her third counseling interview:

MRS. ALBUM: We've been talking and talking but I don't see that it has made any difference. I still don't have an orgasm with my husband.

MR. NUNN: You think this is the goal of therapy for you?

MRS. ALBUM: Well, shouldn't I expect this? Men get their pleasure, why should a woman be denied hers?

MR. NUNN: This reminds me of what we have talked about in some of our previous discussions (*pause*)—that is, you have piled up much resentment against men. You told me your brother could do everything, but your father would not let you do anything. Then you talked about the way your husband seems to enjoy life but you do not enjoy yours.

MRS. ALBUM: Well, I don't! That was the reason for those affairs I told you about. I thought I should have as much enjoyment in life as he has.

MR. NUNN: Let me see if I understand. Are you saying that he had some affairs and that you were going to do the same?

MRS. ALBUM: No, no, no. That's what makes me so furious. He doesn't *have* to do that. He can get his satisfaction in marriage. But I have to *work* for mine. I've always been on the short end of things. He wouldn't understand.

MR. NUNN: You don't think of him as a very understanding person?

MRS. ALBUM: Oh, in some ways I guess he is. He

does try to get me out of the house—to the church and other places. I guess I should go more often and be more sociable. But what am I driving fifty miles a week for? We see you and drive home, and I am no better.

MR. NUNN: I'm not helping you any more than any of the other people—like your husband or your father?

MRS. ALBUM: Oh, I'm sure you want to help. But when do I get to live my life? When am I going to have the same fun that you men do?

MR. NUNN: You mean in bed?

MRS. ALBUM: Well, wouldn't you say that's the best place?

MR. NUNN: I would say that something is misplaced (*pause*)—ah, I mean that you keep insisting that a good orgasm must be the goal of therapy. I don't know if I can meet those conditions.

This interview was drawn out of files that are twenty years old. In the 1970's, the counselor might have referred Mr. and Mrs. Album to the Reproductive Biology Research Foundation in St. Louis. Dr. William Masters and Virginia Johnson could probably have recommended responsible therapists for sexual dysfunction in any major city of the United States.

THE TENSES OF SEXUALITY

The hatreds of yesterday have bound Mrs. Album to a preoccupation with sexual pleasure today. She has found no release from the past to enjoy the present and she cannot relate the feelings of today to the purposes of tomorrow.

Sex that is bound to the past was a special interest of psychoanalysis. Hysteria, voyeurism, impotence, or the exploits of Don Juan were carefully traced to childhood hang-ups. Dysfunction in the present was a sign of problems in the past.

This etiology of eroticism has now been modified in two respects. First, the universality of Freudian theories is questioned by research studies. It is no longer realistic to generalize from abnormality in the specific area of sex to a comprehensive diagnosis of neurosis. Persons may engage in behavior that is a symptom of neurosis in some people without being a sign of neurosis in everyone.

For example, Dr. Edmund Bergler considered a confirmed homosexual to be a neurotic. He outlined a variety of neurotic patterns that appeared in homosexual patients. But this assumption was shaken by the controlled study of a psychologist—Evelyn Hooker. She found thirty homosexuals not in treatment whom she felt to be reasonably well adjusted. She then matched thirty heterosexual men with the homosexuals for age, education, and I.Q. Each of them was given a battery of psychological tests, and considerable information was obtained on their life histories. Several of Dr. Hooker's most skilled clinical colleagues then analyzed the material without any knowledge of the sexual preferences of the subjects. The conclusions of her colleagues showed no connection between an orientation to homosexual behavior and clinical symptoms of mental illness.[28]

The present adjustments of many homosexual persons is not "abnormal." Their life adjustments can only be questioned when we consider a second alteration of the Freudian theory, which is a new look at the future. In psychoanalysis, the emphasis was upon the past.

Now there are psychiatrists, like Victor Frankl, who urge the patients to commit themselves toward the future. The question of the patient should not be what does the world owe to me from the past, but what can I contribute to the world in the future.

Homosexuality proves to be deficient when it is seen in a time dimension. In a partisan view of the Greenwich Village homosexual scene, *Christopher and Gay,* Wallace Hamilton noted that time has a strange new meaning in the gay community. He told Dr. Matthew Dumont: "For the gay, everyday in a relationship is a net profit against its eventual demise." Homosexual love is separated from heterosexual love by the joy of "straight" love in the future, most especially the possibility of a child.[29]

Sexuality is depersonalized when there is no tomorrow. In a participant study of 350 white suburban "swingers" Gilbert Bartell found that the couples did not deviate in any respect from their white middle-class suburban neighbors except in sexual behavior. They were most careful to keep this area of life secret. They expressed to the researcher their boredom with marriage and reported that swinging gave them a better marital relationship. But the researcher found that the couples were socially inert. "These people do nothing other than swing and watch television." [30]

The more sensitive intellectual group of people who enter swinging soon drop out. They find a loss of identity and an absence of commitment in the groups. The people wish no involvement with each other beyond one evening. They avoid any reference to the future and do not identify themselves in any way with commitments to another meeting. As a result, the switching of husbands and wives becomes a mechanical depersonalized act.

The swinger and the homosexual expect everything they can get out of sex today and despair or fear for tomorrow. They are denied the future rewards of children or stronger and more open relationships. There is a push to go beyond responsible relationships in the present because there may never be another meeting like this one.

Timely sex offers more for less. There is the vibrant memory of events and activities that precede a present time of eroticism, a pleasure in the present that is not made frantic by extraction of everything, and a glow of anticipation for the future. We have more fun today because we have confidence that there will be a tomorrow.

7

Live for Less

G. K. Chesterton once remarked that when some people marry, they gain each other; others only lose themselves.

Those who lose themselves may be quite content. For generations, marriage has been defined as the absorption of one person by another. Women were expected to blend into an institutionalized role. Thomas Nelson Page described these expectations in the classic society of Virginia before the Civil War: "Her life was one long act of devotion—devotion to God, devotion to her husband, devotion to her children, devotion to her servants, to the poor, to humanity.

"Nothing happened in the range of her knowledge that her sympathy did not reach and her charity and wisdom did not ameliorate. She was the head and the foot of the church. . . . The training of her children was her work. She watched over them, inspired them, led them, governed them; her will impelled them; her word to them as to her servants was law. She reaped the reward . . . their sympathy and tenderness were hers always, and they worshiped her." [31]

Worship of the selfless mother was based on the cultural and theological belief that women were the "weaker vessels" of society. They possessed the delicate strengths of modesty, delicacy, loveliness. In all areas of life they must be protected as inferior persons. Bold assertions of equality would bring disaster to the order of marriage and motherhood and dishonor to the brazen female. Only by an admission of her weakness could the virtues of a woman be utilized. There were definite restrictions on the areas of society in which she could make a contribution. The *Quarterly Review* of the Methodist Episcopal Church, South, in 1881 considered the question, "May women preach?" and concluded that nothing could compensate for such a sacrifice of feminine modesty. The place of the woman was in the home, the Sunday school, the missionary society; "this must be guarded tho' the heavens fall!" [32]

So long as inequality is accepted by men and women, a dominant-dependent marriage will be stable and satisfying. But the social forces of the twentieth century have shaken this assumption and raised particular strains in a partner who feels inadequate for equality, as in the case of Mr. and Mrs. Harper.

Mr. Harper said that he came to a marriage counselor because someone must help his wife accept divorce. He explained that adequate funds were in trust for the college education of the two children who were in high school. One boy was married and working. Mr. Harper felt that the children understood his position and, at the same time, would comfort Mrs. Harper and let her know that she was a good mother.

"But," said Mr. Harper, "she isn't the wife I need now. Now I think she's a fine woman. I've always been proud of her character. And I owe much to her. Our business started in a little store that she stocked from some money that her father gave her—ah, she sold a farm that she inherited. Anyway, I've set up enough money for her to be more than repaid, and she gets a comfortable house also.

"You see, doctor, I don't want to hurt her. I just want her to see that my position demands some things that just go beyond her. She lives for the home and the kids. Her only entertainment is of some people that we used to know in Germantown, and her family, once in a while. Well, they're nice people and I'm glad to see them, but for the last year I've been vice-president in charge of sales. I need lots of contacts. In my business, we do lots of entertaining. The choice customers are invited to your house. We bought a new one last year. But Circe won't entertain. She says that she never has drunk liquor and doesn't know how to serve it to others. Gee, imagine a social party for executives with no drinks! I'm not knocking her religion, you understand. I go to church myself. I was raised that way. But in my class some things are different now. You understand?"

The counselor promised to see Mrs. Harper. The wife, well dressed and a little plump, could not keep from crying at the beginning of the interview. She felt so hurt and surprised. All her life had been given to Harold (Mr. Harper) and the children. She knew that she could not keep up with the life he now led, with travel, entertainment, and conversation that were beyond her interests. But she had thought that loyalty and affection would keep them together. Now she knew that he was interested in another woman and she could not compete: "I mean, his other woman can mix drinks and talk with important people and likes to travel and all that. I guess she must be very attractive." Mrs. Harper stared hopelessly at the desk. She didn't look away from the counselor; she just looked into the space beside him.

This couple finally made a settlement. Mr. Harper asked the children from time to time about their mother: "How is she taking this business of being divorced?" The children, as Mrs. Harper reported to the counselor, would side with the mother in her grief, but could not condemn their father. They seemed to understand that husband and wife parted because of his business. This was where they placed the blame.

There is much more that could be explored in the life of Mr. and Mrs. Harper, including his denial of his background and the dangers of unchecked ambition. But enough has been revealed to let us know how traditional marriage can disintegrate in an upwardly mobile society, which assumes that husband and wife will rise together.

Lowering the Expectations

Mr. Harper is looking for an adequate partner, the equal of his friends. Our modern assumption is that the woman (or man) must meet that expectation. I have argued thus far that a couple can be equal and that twentieth-century society makes this possible. Those who have more can make the new marriage go.

But there are two limitations to this continual push

for adequacy. The first is that success in society is fleeting. Mr. Harper may abandon the excess baggage of his first wife in his climb to the presidency, but upon whom will he lean if his company is incorporated into a larger conglomerate? His position might be phased out. What kind of wife would help him then?

I was younger when I talked to Mr. Harper and I did not challenge him on a limitation of life that I had not recognized for myself. At that time I was disgusted with his transgression of a covenant relationship. He had left loyalty and love for pleasure and prestige. Or so I saw the situation then.

Now I might be less preoccupied with judgment and more concerned with wisdom. What does Mr. Harper have to look forward to? Has he considered the realistic limitations of ambition? How will he react to forces beyond his control: sickness, death, forced retirement? A thirty-year-old counselor doesn't think much about those things, and neither did the fifty-year-old business executive. The difference between us was that he was old enough to know better, and didn't.

After a few of these failures in counseling, I began to redefine personal adequacy. Self-affirmation became less of a professional product and more of an integration of virtues: courage, humility, wisdom. Loyalty became as significant as craftsmanship.

I finally learned to lower certain expectations of myself and of other people. When I saw the same problem in others, I began to think that marriage should be built on some new definitions. The abilities of a mate as presented in the last twenty years of popular literature would be a challenge even to Mr. Harper. There was too much striving, competition.

One of the events that opened this insight was a conversation with Mrs. Summer. She was executive secretary to the owner of the only large business in her county. In this man she saw an adequacy that was missing in her husband. The boss was bright, aggressive, strong. He was happy with his family and acted as a gentleman toward Mrs. Summer. Mrs. Summer, who had just passed the age of thirty, was fascinated by her contacts with him and frustrated by the comparisons with her own spouse:

MRS. SUMMER: Jake is O.K., you know, but he just doesn't have any get up and go. I mean, when I ask him about what he's going to make of himself, he looks surprised. He says that he likes his job and is glad that we live in a nice house near our families and friends. Oh, it is so boring!

COUNSELOR: He's boring? Or the town? What?

MRS. SUMMER: The whole thing, except for Mr. Bailey and some of his friends that I met on a business trip to Memphis. It was a convention and I set up the booth for our business. Gee, I could hardly go to sleep at night, thinking about the conversations I had with some people who stopped by. I really had to think to talk with some of those men.

COUNSELOR: But not with Jake.

MRS. SUMMER: Nope. (*Grins.*) You must think I'm terrible. Really, I haven't done anything bad—you know, like people look for in small towns. I'm still married to my husband. (*Frowns.*)

COUNSELOR: Ah, any problems there—

MRS. SUMMER: Where?

COUNSELOR: Like, ah, is he adequate as a man?

MRS. SUMMER: I suppose so. I don't have anything

else to compare it with. (*Pause.*) It's O.K. He's a good father. When he comes home, he takes the boy out in the yard and they play for an hour. Then he comes in and smiles and wants to know what we're having for supper. Sometimes he talks about a ball game, or some friend. (*Sigh.*)

COUNSELOR: Which bores you?

MRS. SUMMER: I've already told you that. You act almost as sleepy as he is. He just sits and nods and says "yes" to everything. Gee, what a difference it is to talk with men who have something to say—and are going someplace!

COUNSELOR: Which you are not?

MRS. SUMMER: I guess not. What can I do? I don't want to leave Joey [the son] and I don't want to hurt Jake. But there's just nothing in my marriage!

COUNSELOR: Nothing?

MRS. SUMMER: Well, suppose you were stuck in this like me? It's fine for you to sit in a nice office and talk about how things are out in the boondocks, but just try living there. Would you?

COUNSELOR: I don't know. But I do see some wives who wish they had a husband with the qualities of yours.

MRS. SUMMER: Like what?

COUNSELOR: Well, like playing with your son, or smiling at you, or being content to come home in the evening.

MRS. SUMMER: I'm not knocking him. Jake has some good points.

COUNSELOR: He might have one that you've missed.

MRS. SUMMER: Well, I didn't drive 50 miles to play games. Tell me what it is, doctor.

COUNSELOR: He's more patient than I could be with an ambitious woman who might be hard to live with at times.

MRS. SUMMER: Meaning me? (*I nod. She is silent for thirty seconds.*) How do you know this? (*I raise an eyebrow.*) O.K. I push pretty hard for what I want. But how can I get him stirred up a little more?

I had no adequate answer for Mrs. Summer, except to suggest that Mr. Summer come in with her for the next interview, which he didn't. I guess that most of the benefits of that interview came to me. I began to see that adequacy in marriage might consist of virtues that run deep, and therefore steady and long-lasting. Faith, hope, love are not easily acquired, or shaken. They survive ambition, fear, failure, boredom.

When we look for more enduring talents in a marriage we can be content with some inadequacies in the present. Does it really matter that a wife cannot mix drinks or a husband engage in stimulating conversation?

The answer to those questions will depend more on our own adequacy than on that of our mate. A self-actualized person is not bored. He carries his own conversations around in his head. He has a natural curiosity that excites him in humdrum as well as in exotic surroundings.

An adequate person is not shaken by some minor social deficiency in a mate, since he does not think that he needs that kind of support to compete in business or to gain acceptance in his profession. He does not expect an intimate relationship to compensate for his inadequacies.

I do not mean to suggest that husband and wife learn nothing from each other, or that they should expect complete self-sufficiency. If so, why be married? I am only warning against extractive relationships in which one person becomes dissatisfied because the partner does not provide an answer to boredom, immaturity, insecurity, and ineptitude.

What, then, can we expect in an intimate relationship between equals? This brings us to the second limitation on adequacy, which is a tempering of our expectations with love.

Love in marriage is an exclusive devotion that subdues the antagonisms inherent in the living together of two different people. In the context of this discussion, it is a belief and a practice of growth by association rather than a hope that deficiencies will be met through blending into the life of another. We are attracted to rather than driven to each other.

Friendship marriage has a certain detached quality of love. We enjoy each other without great need for the partner. Most of our basic needs in life have already been satisfied if we are adequate people. We do not expect another to fill us up. There is more affirmation of the other, therefore, and less preoccupation with possession.

Love based on adequacy can take or leave some of the elements of romance that sound so essential in song and novel. Sex, mutual reassurance, constant acts of devotion are not so omnipresent in the relaxed atmosphere around a couple who admire each other more than they require from the other. The teen-age friends of my daughters smile at my habit of patting both my daughters and wife when I'm in the house (I used to do it some in public, until I saw a wedding picture in which a colleague had unconsciously draped his hand low on the back of his wife as they moved through the receiving line). But I don't think that my family would fall apart if I didn't stroke them five times a day. I enjoy patting them because I think they are cute and my father taught me to express general affection by his clamping his hand on my shoulder when he came home from work or rubbing my head as he sat down at the dinner table.

Doing Without Defenses

If we expect to extract less from our partner and are not anxious about what we can give to the other, then we do not need to hide our true selves. The adequate partner will not take anything away from us—it isn't needed—and will not leave if some of our inadequacies show.

Suppose the partner expects us to meet some of his (her) needs, do we still hide? Mr. Park (Chapter 3), faced that problem with his wife whom he thought to be most inadequate. He felt the burden of keeping peace in the house when her nerves were on edge, of shining through her depression with cheerful thoughts for her, or of positive reassurances to the children.

But after Mr. and Mrs. Park had talked to their therapists for several months, Mr. Park said: "I used to think I had to hold everything together. Yes, I did. Ha! Boy, was I a big shot. (*Smiles.*) I guess our talks convinced me that my wife could do some things for herself, and that the kids could get along with her better than I thought. So now I take it a little easier. So long as she doesn't really blow up with them, I let them work some things out. I may give some advice now and then, but its aimed at helping them to work it out themselves. I used to rush in and take all the responsibility myself. I think you said that all that did was to keep her dependence going, right?"

Mr. Park has more respect for the adequacy of his wife and children and less concern for his own capacity to meet every need. He no longer has to act as though he could take care of everything. "I've even learned to let my face show my disappointment when they are quarreling or when I don't get the answer I want. I guess it's just a feeling that every tub will have to stand on its own bottom in our family—you ever heard that phrase before?"

The attitude of Mr. Park does not imply irresponsibility. He is really enjoying his responsibilities more. With a new respect for his family and fewer expectations of himself, he can blend care, respect, and responsibility. He is acting more as a friend and less the role of ever-present protector, which was his traditional understanding of "husband" and "father." He is getting more out of his marriage because he is demanding less.

8

Understand Each Season

We can live for less when we know what counts the most. A marriage that matures is built on a philosophy of life. As the seasons of the family change, we should be more aware of the values that endure.

The values of life appear in the cycle of the family: early marital adjustment, responsibility for children and to society, the "empty nest," and aging. In each of these seasons, love and friendship take on new meaning.

Satisfaction by Season

The satisfactions of a companionship marriage were measured by interviews with 852 married couples in Syracuse, New York, in 1960. Boyd C. Rollins and Harold Feleman considered positive friendship to be demonstrated by laughing together, calm discussions as a couple, stimulating exchange of ideas, and working together on a project.

Both husbands and wives saw growth in companionship from the beginning of marriage to the preschool age of children. Then there was a leveling off. The low point of marital satisfaction came as children were launched from the home. After the nest was empty, companionship was more positive and continued to increase, with an apparent temporary setback just before the husband retires.[33]

Each stage in this cycle of life will call for some variation on the theme of intimacy and equality. In the development of these themes, loving and liking become one. There is a blending of *erōs* and *philia* as the marriage matures.

In the early phase of marriage, there are some conscious differences between loving and liking. The couple must consider the new requirements of equality for man and woman against a background of traditional matrimony. Individuality must be discovered and respected in an aura of romance and yearning to be "one flesh."

This is the season for self-awareness. It is typically the opportunity to apply the first advice of friendship marriage—possess yourself. Possession of another must be tempered by the characteristics of equalitarian intimacy: deliberate choice of the mate, valuing of another as having your own values, mutuality of admiration rather than social pressure to stay together, and sharing of competence.

Self-possession cuts convention. The traditional expectations of the male dominance of an inferior female are no longer required. A couple can be intimately related and still be equal.

But this liberty must be tempered with responsibility. In Chapter 6 we considered the limitations of time upon sexuality in marriage. Neither sex nor the marriage has a future without regard for a past that engenders faith and a present that is filled with hope. We surrender to each other because we know there are boundaries that will not be broken. Freedom is the must fun in faithful people.

"Sex for tomorrow" assumes the satisfaction of long-term values: faith, hope, love. Instant gratification is subdued by realistic appraisal of self-respect, gratitude for affection, trust for the children. The boundaries of monogamy are maintained by convictions that cause each partner to value the other as a trusted friend along with the delights of a lover.

When the satisfactions of friendship and romance are met in one relationship, there is less need to talk about these elements of marriage, or even to discuss the relationship itself. Besides, by this time the couple is probably busy with the myriad demands of parenthood. The man and wife have entered a new level of intimate equality.

Caring with Confidence

Love, for the newly married, is the building of devotion despite the tensions of dominance-submission, identity-equality. Identity is maintained in intimacy.

One hope of this love is children, or opportunities to act as father or mother to the "little ones" of this world. The sense of parental obligation may be met with one's own offspring, or in cheerful association with neighborhood waifs, or younger or older people in need.

With the coming of this responsibility, love becomes caring. Compassion is now as significant as passion.

There is less impulse-gratification and more planning for the future. Faithfulness takes on new meaning as mutual responsibility. Hope becomes a belief that some sacrifices in the present will become future pride in the character of children or accomplishment of pupils.

These growing requirements of love snap some marriages and sap others. The "snap" in the marriage of Mr. and Mrs. Lake (Chapter 5) occurred more than a year before their divorce decree. For several years there had been a growing realization that he expected more than she could bear. He expected his children to be well behaved and his wife to be cheerful and competent. She looked for inner strength and found none. Only her guilt increased.

"Responsibility" was the club of Mr. Lake and the curse of his wife. He knew how to manage employees; why couldn't she manage the household? With more of these questions, the resentment and guilt of Mrs. Lake boiled over into tantrums, followed by depression. She expected herself to be competent, and this increased the frustration. In one interview she said: "I really don't like men. I mean, they posture so much as important people. They seem to need women to look up to them. I can do anything a man can do. But why can't I control my feelings like my husband? I don't think a man has it any harder, or is stronger. So why can't I sail over my troubles like he does?"

Mrs. Lake expected a companionship marriage between equals, but it had not developed in the early days of their life together and now it was a question that split them under the strain of responsibility.

In a more hopeful marriage, like that of Mr. and Mrs. Park (Chapter 3), confidence and compassion grow with the requirements of parenthood. Mr. Park learned new ways of relating to his wife and this changed his attitude on the job. He discovered that acceptance of some share in family living did not require omnipotence. He didn't have to solve every quarrel or have an answer for every problem. Husband and wife could cooperate without loss of self-competence.

The Necessity of Wisdom

As children grow and move out into the world, parents have visible evidence of their strengths and weaknesses. The imperfections of personality and the limitations of circumstances cannot be denied. Some early choices in marriage can now be traced to fruition in success or disaster.

These were some thoughts of Mr. and Mrs. Gaston as they surveyed a conventional marriage. Mrs. Gaston had traded social approval for respect from her children; now she feels cheated. Mr. Gaston gave up self-respect for economic and community security; when he had enough, he wanted out. He realized that he really didn't like his wife; she was aware that the children really didn't like her. (Mrs. Gaston never thought of liking or loving her husband; he was an actor who played a part with her.)

Mr. and Mrs. Gaston began in middle age to ask if their goals were satisfying. What are the values that build a lasting relationship on strong character?

The asking of this question is a prelude to satisfaction in the later years of life. A stable answer will give integrity to the overall experience of life; we will make sense out of some of the nonsense that we created or that others foisted upon us.

Wisdom is the ability to integrate our human problems into a workable, comprehensive picture that includes love, faith, hope, evil, and disaster. It recognizes the growing limitations of physical performance without diminishing the significance of character and decision. The great value of this process is an ability to simplify life, to lay aside the unessential elements and conserve strength for that which really counts in life.[34]

What counts? Mr. Gaston counted the cost of economic security and felt cheated. He would gladly have replaced money with "regard for people." Most especially, he wanted a woman who would care about him as a person, someone who would share affection. Mrs. Gaston knew well the price of her marriage, and would threaten her husband with financial ruin whenever he thought of divorce. As the two looked back over the years, they saw possessions and position looming over people and relationships.

Mr. Park, on the other hand, decided for people, including himself. The value of personal relations grew as he came to appreciate the contributions of father, mother, and brothers to his own character and confidence. Now in gratitude, and with some humility, he began to cherish individuality in himself, his wife, and his children. The family was no longer an enterprise to be managed (as it was for Mr. Lake), but an intimate association of loved ones who had ideas, and idiosyncracies of their own.

I would not want to draw too severe a choice between people and things. Mr. Park could supply the necessary material possessions for his family; his choice was of an attitude, a way of looking at people. He was not faced with the dilemma of Mr. Gaston, who would have lost his business if he renounced a wife whom he did not like.

If we were to develop a formula for life, would we not place people above possessions? Possessions are significant but are subsidiary to personal relationship-ships.

Another part of wisdom is to place character above personality, conscience above ego. This is the severe test of early marriage, to remain an individual without being selfish, to share without suffering. The modern emphasis upon immediate gratification and boundless equality intensifies this struggle. Many young couples separate because self-gratification is incomplete. Accommodation to the needs of another is unacceptable. They ask what others can give to them rather than what both can give to life together. Our long analysis of friendship in marriage is an attempt to meet this modern dilemma. Intimacy and equality can be combined when there are values in our life: faith, hope, love.

Mrs. Polk (Chapter 4) was caught in this dilemma until her thirties. Then she looked openly at the limitations on her creativity that came with loyalty to a passive husband. Her final decision was that her husband meant enough to her for the marriage to continue. She would not tell him all his inadequacies and would begin to appreciate his strengths.

I do not know how Mrs. Summer (Chapter 7) solved the temptation to build her ego at the expense of her marriage. When I saw her, the bright and sophisticated world of her boss was more appealing than the same old smile of her husband and his contented presence in the evening. Maybe faith and love would prove more valuable than excitement and clever conversation, but who knows? Some talented people take an ego trip and others accept the dictates of conscience.

Both Mrs. Summer and Mrs. Polk were caught up in another criterion of wisdom: creativity above convention. Their problem was to keep a conventional marriage and still be creative. Both women found some solution in their jobs, but marriage was still a drag. In both instances their husbands would have accepted equality with the woman; only the wives didn't think their husbands were their equal!

One solution to that dilemma is to establish priorities. Does brilliant conversation come before steadfast love? Is aggressive competition in the business world more important than kindness and affection in the home? Certainly these attractive women could be comfortable with more talented men, but would that be worth the sacrifice of other values that would be more dependable and enduring?

I have weighed my answer on the side of enduring values. I have argued for equality, but with limitations. The intimacy of marriage creates fixed obligations that alter the form of friendship. Friendship in marriage is a controlled relationship. We only give part of ourselves to a partner, but that part binds us by faith and hope to a loving and satisfying union. The bond is not a competitive one that can be renegotiated whenever we experience a handicap on our personal ambitions.

My cautions on creativity should not be interpreted as sanctions for the Gastons' ceaseless search for security. Those who live for convention above all else are handicapped people. Caution has calcified their communication; they are hardly aware of the puppet role they play.

But suppose a partner were more adequate than Mr. Gaston and found himself struggling with a conventional marriage. Should he abandon the wife who was satisfying to him in less successful days and obtain the benefits of a more socially adequate partner?

Mr. Harper decided for another partner, but with decent compassion for his faithful, bucolic wife. Ah, if only she had grown with him in intellect and social acumen! But her virtues had no high cash value. In fact, they would be valuable to Mr. Harper only in case of a social or psychological recession. If he should suffer misfortune, illness, or some other handicap, then he would prize the steadfast love of a rather stolid mate. But for the present he does not anticipate any disaster —and the diminishing of his potency seems far distant.

Mr. Harper has missed the key to wisdom in middle age—a sense of the eternal. This is the criterion for simplifying life, as we inevitably face a decline in our energy. We can no longer try everything, hold on to all for which we have fought and won in life. What will we give up? What must go?

The wise partner builds eternal values into his present marriage so that the question is answered long before circumstances wrench some long-treasured goal from him. The receding satisfaction may be public recognition, salary, control of lands and leases, sexual performance, personal features and proportions, domination of children, or keenness of the senses. We can't hold them—for long.

Figure out what will last before it is too late for the decisions to be under your control. No one likes to let go at the last minute. Too much energy is expended in trying to keep that which is slipping away! A more economical expenditure of energy would begin with some calculations. What is worth keeping and how do I cut loose from the nonessentials?

We cut loose when we see our values clearly. Mr.

Park relaxed his hold on business success and personal ambition when he incorporated compassion and charity into his life. These were values worth the struggle. The desire for unfettered creativity faded for Mrs. Polk when she weighed it against the reliable relationship she was developing with her husband. These people came to know themselves well enough to make realistic choices, which were rewarded by more lasting satisfaction.

But what if the choices do not bring swift satisfaction? Mr. Park faced that question. His wife was not immediately cheerful because he became less possessive. There still were moody days and sudden explosions. Neither obtained perfection overnight. In fact, it would be disaster for Mr. Park to think that a change on his part must be tied to a quick response from his wife, or vice versa. He was urged to act differently for his *own* sake. Such a change would benefit his family, but if they didn't react, he was still to affirm his new insights. Neither he nor anyone else should abandon a new strength of character because there is no external reinforcement. The goal is inner satisfaction.

The power of that inner satisfaction is a living faith. For some very adequate persons that faith is completely in themselves. But for most of us there must be some trust in a strength beyond ourselves. We place the eternal above the temporal because of gratitude for the steadfast love of God. It is his approval that rewards us. We possess ourselves because we surrender only to a divine being. No other total surrender is appropriate. We cut convention for the sake of a faith and a hope that penetrate the external social fabric of a small town or the conformity to company expectations of an executive's wife.

Only the values that endure beyond this life can lead us to enjoy life more when we live for "less." Faith, hope, and love hold us steadfast and satisfied through every season of companionship. Romance (*erōs*) and friendship (*philia*) are the twin loves that are united in the greater love of God (*agāpe*). The life and power of his Son guide our decisions for people above possessions, character above ego, creativity above convention, eternal above temporal. The ultimate ability to like the one we love comes from One who loves us, whether we are likable or not.

Notes

1. Ernest R. Mowrer, "The Differentiation of Husband and Wife Roles," *Journal of Marriage and the Family*, Aug., 1969, pp. 534–540.

2. Anne Steinmann and David Fox, "Specific Areas of Agreement and Conflict in Women's Self Perception," *Journal of Marriage and the Family*, May, 1969, pp. 281–289.

3. *Atlanta Constitution*, Jan. 1, 1973, p. 21–B.

4. Lee Kanowitz, *Women and the Law: The Unfinished Revolution* (University of New Mexico Press, 1969).

5. Nena and George O'Neill, *Open Marriage: A New Life Style for Couples* (J. B. Lippincott Company, 1972).

6. Irving Tallman, "Working Class Wives in Suburbia: Fulfillment or Crisis?" *Journal of Marriage and the Family*, Feb., 1969, pp. 65–72.

7. *Psychology Today*, July, 1970, p. 43.

8. *Ibid.*, p. 41.

9. *Ibid.*, p. 52.

10. *Psychology Today*, Aug., 1969, pp. 24, 26.

11. Gerald Gurin *et al.*, *Americans View Their Mental Health* (Basic Books, Inc., Publishers, 1960), pp. 113–114.

12. Joann and Jack DeLora (eds.), *Intimate Life Styles: Marriage and Its Alternatives* (Goodyear Publishing Co., Inc., 1972) p. 169.

13. John F. Cuber and Peggy B. Harroff, *The Significant Americans: A Study of Sexual Behavior Among the Affluent* (Appleton-Century-Crofts, 1965).

14. Ezra Stotland, *The Psychology of Hope* (Jossey-Bass, Inc., Publishers, 1969), p. 145.

15. *Ibid.*, p. 154.

16. Nena and George O'Neill, *Open Marriage,* p. 257.

17. "Do You Mary and June and Beverly and Ruth Take These Men?" *Psychology Today,* Jan., 1972, p. 58.

18. Erik Erikson, *Insight and Responsibility* (W. W. Norton and Company, Inc., 1964), p. 116.

19. Murray Bowen, "A Family Concept of Schizophrenia," in *The Etiology of Schizophrenia,* ed. by Donald Jackson (Basic Books, Inc., Publishers, 1960), Ch. 6.

20. Joann and Jack DeLora (eds.), *Intimate Life Styles,* p. 403.

21. George R. Fitzgerald, *Communes* (Paulist/Newman Press, 1971).

22. See I Cor. 6:12–20, and D. S. Bailey, *The Mystery of Love and Marriage* (Harper & Brothers, 1952), pp. 50–54.

23. *Time,* Sept. 10, 1973, p. 48.

24. Joann and Jack DeLora (eds.), *Intimate Life Styles,* pp. 93–94.

25. I Peter 3:7; Gal. 3:28.

26. John W. Hudson and Lura S. Henze, "Campus Values in Mate Selection: A Replication," in Joann and Jack DeLora (eds.), *Intimate Life Styles,* p. 3.

27. Ira Reiss, "The Sexual Renaissance: A Summary and Analysis," *Journal of Social Issues,* April, 1966. For a summary of research studies and debates, see Kenneth L. Canon and Richard Long, "Premarital Sexual Behavior in the Sixties," *Journal of Marriage and the Family,* Feb., 1971, pp. 36–49.

28. Martin Hoffman, "Homosexual," *Psychology Today,* July, 1969, pp. 43–45.

29. *Psychotherapy and Social Sciences Review,* July 21, 1973, p. 30.

30. Gilbert D. Bartell, "Group Sex Among the Mid Americans," in Joann and Jack DeLora (eds.), *Intimate Life Styles,* p. 298.

31. Ann B. Scott, "Women, Religion and Social Change in the South 1830–1930," in Samuel S. Hill, Jr., and others, *Religion and the Solid South* (Abingdon Press, 1972), p. 94.

32. *Ibid.,* p. 104.

33. Boyd C. Rollins and Harold Feleman, "Marital Satisfaction Over the Family Life Cycle," *Journal of Marriage and the Family,* Feb., 1970, pp. 20–28.

34. These ideas are drawn from Erik Erikson, *Insight and Responsibility* (W. W. Norton & Company, Inc., 1964), pp. 127–134; and Lewis J. Sherrill, *The Struggle of the Soul* (The Macmillan Company, 1963), pp. 157–185.